cooking with
aristos

contents

cooking with
aristos

This book is dedicated to my maternal grandfather Steve Fradelos, my mother Athena and my father and mentor George.

Published in Australia by Random House Australia Pty. Ltd.
20 Alfred Street, Milsons Point, NSW Australia 2061
http://www.randomhouse.com.au

Sydney New York Toronto London Auckland Johannesburg and agencies throughout the world

First published in 2002

National Library of Australia
Cataloguing-in-Publication Data

Papandroulakis, Aristos.
Cooking with Aristos

Includes index
ISBN 1 74051 454 8 (pbk.).

1. Papandroulakis family. 2. Cookery. 3. Quick and easy cookery. 4. Restaurateurs - Australia. I. Title

641.5

Portrait photographer: Jason Capobianco
Food photographer: Ian Wallace
Props: Ashisha Cunningham
Food technician/ Home economist: Justine Poole
Art direction and design: Anne Marie Cummins and Justin Thomas
  for uber creative pty ltd
Production manager: Angela Alegounarias
Publishing co-ordinator: Anabel Pandiella
Editorial Assistance: Alexandra Black, Jan Hutchinson and Scott Ellis
Publisher: James Mills-Hicks

Film separation by Response Colour Graphics Pty. Ltd, Sydney and
Pica Digital (PTE) Limited, Singapore
Printed by Tien Wah Press (PTE) Limited, Singapore

introduction

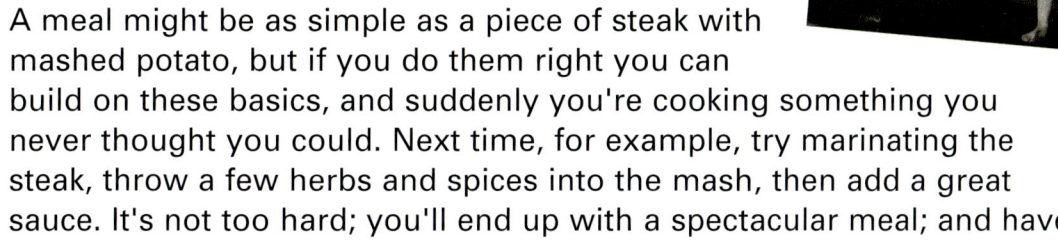

The challenge in cooking for television is to take some simple ingredients, whatever I find, and turn them into something special. It might look difficult (and sometimes it can be) but I love doing it because it's the way I was taught to cook. It follows one of the most fundamental rules of the kitchen, something my dad taught me when I first started out and which I still stick to: Learn the basics, learn to do them well, then work from there.

A meal might be as simple as a piece of steak with mashed potato, but if you do them right you can build on these basics, and suddenly you're cooking something you never thought you could. Next time, for example, try marinating the steak, throw a few herbs and spices into the mash, then add a great sauce. It's not too hard; you'll end up with a spectacular meal; and have a lot of fun as well!

Apply the same rule to sauces, which can transform a meal. I can tell you now that for all the different sauces around, almost all come from five basic recipes. If you learn to make those — and I've included instructions for each — then moving up a step is easy because you've got a great foundation to work from. Start with the basics, use your imagination and experiment as you go. You'll have your own signature sauce before you know it.

The recipes on these pages have come from a range of different places. Some are from my family and haven't changed from the time I first learnt them, and others are just things I experimented with and improved along the way.

But no matter where they're from, they all still follow that first rule: You start with something simple and make it something special. Even with the ingredients, I've tried to show you ways to take ordinary things and turn them into a meal to remember.

I hope you will enjoy cooking these dishes as much as I have through the years!

Aristos

life in the kitchen

Scenes from our family restaurant, the Rex Café in Bunbury, where I first learnt to cook.

When I think about it, there wasn't much question about me becoming a chef — it was in my blood!

My mother's family opened their first restaurant in Bunbury, Western Australia in 1935 and that was where my father found a job in 1960 when he arrived in Perth as a chef in the Merchant Navy. He'd jumped ship and was at the Greek Club when a call came through asking if anyone knew of a chef looking for work. He took off for Bunbury, got the job, and before long he met and fell in love with the bosses' daughter.

That was enough for him to decide Australia was where he wanted to be. He went back to Greece and migrated officially about six months later. Mum and dad were married soon after that, then I came along. So when they took over my grandfather's restaurant that's where I grew up, spending most of my time in the kitchen watching my parents and grandparents as they prepared the food. I learnt everything I could along the way.

Even when I was a little kid I knew I wanted to be just like my dad. Mum remembers finding me once in the big flour bin. When she pulled me out the first thing I said was: **"Mum! I want to be a cook!"** And I haven't changed my mind since!

As I grew up I was still hanging around in the kitchen as much as I could. I used to get my mates over and we'd play in the store room (and pinch a few soft drinks when nobody was looking!) but all the time I was watching what my dad was doing.

By the time I was ten years old I was helping out with washing the dishes. Later on, when my mates were getting ready to go out on Friday and Saturday nights, I'd be in the kitchen cleaning squid, trying to cut the fish and doing the little things I could like garnishing the plates ... and loving it!

It was in the restaurant kitchen that I got my first real chance to try cooking, when I was still just a teenager.

On some afternoons dad would go out with a few mates, then come back and doze in the corner for a couple of hours while things were quiet. I was supposed to keep an eye on things and wake him up when it got busy or if the fishermen came in with the catch ... but I decided I wouldn't.

The produce would arrive and I'd start preparing the food. Then later the customers would come in and I'd quietly keep going. Eventually dad would wake up, take a look at me and ask: "So? It's been pretty quiet?" And I'd point over at the pile of dirty plates.

My dad was always very careful to make sure things were just right. He'd be out the kitchen door checking with customers to see if everything was fine, and when it was he'd break into a big smile and tell them: **"My son cooked that!" I was about 14 years old.**

Like I said, I'd always wanted to be just like my dad. He was one of those people who took real pride in making sure things were done properly and that people in his kitchen really cared about what they were making.

The first thing I said was: "Mum! I want to be a cook!" And I haven't changed my mind since!

In the early years my great grandfather and dad were an inspiration. Today my dad's still showing me what to do!

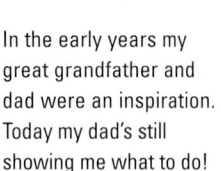

I knew if I wanted to be a really good chef, I'd have to do the same. So I watched dad closely and learnt how to do the ordering, how to choose the best fish and the best cuts of meat, how to prepare them and how to make sure the customer was always happy. Because I was doing the ordering from such a young age I learnt early on about produce and how to deal with butchers and fishermen. Believe me, the best way to learn is to buy bad cuts — you don't do that again!

For the next few years I kept at it in the kitchen, learning the trade secrets, experimenting a bit myself (usually when Dad wasn't looking!) and just taking it all in. **Everyone in the family had little tips or tricks, recipes or skills** which I tried to pick up. My grandfather, for example, would put his heart into something as simple as cleaning a fish. He was pedantic about the fillets being perfect and, no kidding, when there was a stack of fish prepared by different people, you could go through and pick out which ones had been done by him — he was that thorough.

Then there were certain dishes dad cooked and some that mum cooked. Even today if I call them to say I'm coming over and ask for something special, like some Gravy Beef, dad will say: "I'll get your mum to do that.''

I watched everyone and tried to pick up who did what, and how they did it. I changed the recipes a little bit, but to be honest, I hardly need to have bothered. When they did it they got it right!

Food played such a huge part in our lives. I learnt how to prepare and eat different things when they were in season or when they were in their prime. I learnt to build a good rapport with the butcher. I still go to his shop without a clue what I'm going to buy and just pick what is best on the day or what he advises me is good.

I learnt to buy fish with my eyes. If it looks good, chances are it is. Try it yourself next time you're buying fish — whichever one looks bright, shiny and has a good lustre will generally be the best. Even if you don't know fish, 99 percent of the time you'll be spot on!

As well as the restaurant, my parents had four fish and chip shops, a Souvlaki shop and a lunch bar, so there was a lot of different food being prepared, talked about and eaten. I was learning all the time.

By the time I was 20, when my parents sold the restaurant, I knew that cooking was what I wanted to do in life. I tried a couple of other jobs, but at 26 I opened my own restaurant.

These days I still spend most of my time in the kitchen. My dad drops in from time to time to take a look at what I'm doing and offer a bit of advice — even when I don't need it! My brother is there working with me too, and even a few of the regular characters from the old restaurant come and visit us.

Some days when I look out from the kitchen I get a real feeling of déjà vu. It's the same way of life I can always remember, but what can I say … **I'm still loving it!**

entrées

It's great to have my brother working with me in the kitchen.

entrées

Strathan and I are pretty typical brothers. We fight and argue now and again but I love him and it's great to work with him in a kitchen … well, most of the time. I'm a pretty passionate guy and I admit I can be temperamental, but I honestly think he's worse! I might blow up if something annoys me, but then I forget about it. Strathan will hold a grudge for a week, or at least until payday.

He was a bit of a late starter as a chef — he qualified in 2001 — but he has one great ability I envy. **He can look at a recipe once and remember it forever.** We were in the kitchen one day and I walked over to see what he was

making. There were bits and pieces everywhere, but I couldn't see a cookbook.

Eventually I asked him: "Where's the recipe?" He shrugged. "Oh, I read it," he said. "Where'd you read it?" I persisted. "Oh, at the doctor's surgery," he replied, without even looking up. At the doctor's! Suddenly I'm playing the worried big brother. He was at the doctor? What was wrong? Was he sick? When was he at the doctor? He just kept on working: "No, don't panic," he said. "It was about three years ago." **That's my brother...**

olive pâté

Ingredients
400g (14 oz) black pitted olives
1 tablespoon lemon juice
⅓ cup olive oil

Method
Blend olives in food processor until smooth. Add lemon juice and continue to process until well combined. While processor is running, slowly drizzle in the oil in small amounts until the mixture begins to thicken. Once it has started to thicken, add the remaining oil in a thin steady stream. Season with pepper to taste. This will keep in sterilised containers in the fridge for up to 6 months.

Aristos' Tip: Use to spread on pizza bases and top with sundried tomatoes or spread on foccacia and top with roasted capsicum and cheese.

grilled field mushrooms

Ingredients
8 large mushrooms, stems removed
pepper
salt
splash of balsamic vinegar
8 small balls of bocconcini cheese,
   thinly sliced
1 sprig of fresh lemon thyme

Method
Place mushrooms on a baking tray, stem side down. Place under grill for about 15 minutes or until mushrooms begin to soften. Remove tray from grill and place mushrooms stem side up on a dish. Season with black pepper, salt and a splash of balsamic vinegar to taste. Allow to sit for 1 hour.
   Place mushrooms on a baking tray and top with bocconcini cheese and a small sprig of lemon thyme. Grill until cheese melts.
   Serve immediately.
Serves 4

seafood chowder

Ingredients
1 x 500g (1lb) fish fillet, perch or
   snapper
2l (3⅓ pints) fish stock
240g (8½oz) butter
240g (8½oz) self raising flour
2 carrots
3 sticks of celery
¼ cabbage
60g (2oz) butter, extra
1 potato
2 x 375g (13fl oz) tins of carnation milk
salt
pepper

Method
Chop carrots, celery and cabbage into medium-size dice and cook in the extra butter for 5-7 minutes. Add the fish pieces and cook for a further 3 minutes, then remove from heat.
   Peel and chop the potato into medium-size dice and boil until cooked. Set aside. Add the boiling stock to the roux and whisk until of a smooth consistency. Stir in both cans of carnation milk and stir well. Simmer for 20 minutes until the taste of the flour has gone and the soup has thickened. Add salt and pepper to taste.
   Remove from heat and if there are any lumps in the chowder strain it through a sieve. Add vegetables and fish and mix well.
   Serve immediately with fresh crusty bread.

Aristos' Tip: Occasionally homemade fish stock can taste a little weak. Crumble some powdered fish stock into the chowder to really boost the flavour if it's tasting bland.

Olive pâté

Barbecued king
prawns

barbecued king prawns

Ingredients

500g (1lb) large king prawns
2 cups (500ml/17½fl oz) white wine
200ml (7fl oz) olive oil
2 garlic cloves, sliced
60g (2oz) fresh basil, finely chopped
salt
pepper

Method

Peel prawns, leaving the heads and tails on, and devein them. Place in a shallow baking dish. In a separate bowl mix white wine, olive oil, garlic, basil, salt and pepper. Pour mixture over prawns and marinate in the fridge for 3 hours.

Heat barbecue and place prawns on the hottest part of the hotplate. Cook for 3 minutes each side, or until the meat has turned white all the way through the prawn.

Serves 4

Aristos' Tip: Another easy way of cooking these prawns is to place them onto a very hot barbecue plate, without peeling or marinating them. Just sprinkle a little salt on them. Cook the prawns for approximately 3 minutes each side, splash 60ml (2fl oz) of Pernod over them and remove from the heat. This marinade can also be used for lobsters, yabbies, Balmain bugs and other shellfish.

baked stuffed avocados

Ingredients

3 avocados
¼ cup (2fl oz) lime juice
salt

For filling

2 cups crabmeat, tuna or
  chicken, flaked
1 cup (250ml/9fl oz) béchamel sauce
  (recipe page 114)
pinch of cayenne pepper
1 tablespoon onion, chopped
2 tablespoons green capsicum,
  chopped
salt
pepper
1 cup cheddar cheese, grated

Method

Preheat oven to 180°C (350°F).

Cut avocados in half lengthways and remove stones. Sprinkle halves with lime juice and salt.

Combine crab meat with béchamel sauce, cayenne pepper, onion and capsicum. Season the mixture with salt and pepper to taste. Fill avocado with mixture and sprinkle grated cheese on top.

Cover the bottom of a baking dish with ½cm of water and arrange avocados on tray. Bake for about 15 minutes or until cheese melts and avocado is heated through.

Serves 6

chicken and vegetable soup

Ingredients

1 chicken
1 onion
2 carrots
1 turnip
1 swede
2 celery sticks
1 parsnip
2 potatoes
60g (2oz) butter
½ cup small macaroni
salt
pepper

Method

Rinse the chicken under the tap and set aside. Wash, peel and roughly chop the vegetables. Melt the butter in a large saucepan and add the vegetables, cooking them for a few minutes and stirring occasionally with a wooden spoon or spatula to stop them sticking.

Place the chicken in the pan with the vegetables and cover with water. Bring to the boil and simmer for 1 hour. Skim and strain the stock through a colander. Remove meat from chicken and chop roughly.

Strain vegetables over a bowl and put them into a blender to make a purée. Pour the stock back into the saucepan and bring back to the boil. Add macaroni. When macaroni is cooked al dente, stir through the vegetable purée and season to taste with salt and pepper. Just before serving, add chicken pieces. Serve piping hot with crusty Italian bread.

Serves 6

cayenne asparagus

Ingredients

8 large asparagus spears
drizzle of olive oil
60g (2oz) of Parmesan, grated or
  shaved
sprinkle of cayenne pepper
1 bunch parsley, tops cut finely and
  placed in water until they curl
1 red capsicum, thinly sliced
splash of balsamic vinegar

Method

To prepare the asparagus, hold the end of the asparagus with one hand and the middle with other and bend the stem until it snaps. Discard woody core end. Quickly blanch in boiling water and remove. Chill immediately in iced water. Pat dry and place asparagus in two lots of 4 spears on a baking tray. Sprinkle with olive oil and Parmesan cheese and grill until cheese browns.

To serve, sprinkle with cayenne pepper and garnish with parsley and capsicum. Drizzle with balsamic vinegar.
Serves 2

Aristos' Tip: Placing vegetables in iced water stops the cooking process and helps to retain their colour and flavour.

figs wrapped in prosciutto

Ingredients

30g (1oz) butter
120ml (4fl oz) white wine
juice of 1 lime
250ml (9fl oz) cream
8 ripe figs, peeled and kept in tact
8 thin slices prosciutto
pepper

Method

In a small saucepan, melt the butter and add the wine, lime juice and cream. Combine well and simmer until the sauce thickens. If the sauce splits, add a little more cream. If the consistency of the sauce is a little thin it can be thickened with a little cornflour and water.

Preheat oven to 200°C (400°F).

Wrap each fig with prosciutto and place on baking tray. Cook in the oven for 5 minutes and then place under the grill for a further 5 minutes. Place figs on a serving plate and pour the sauce over the top.

Serve immediately with a good grinding of pepper.
Serves 4

barbecued lamb fillets with rocket sauce

Ingredients

3 slices stale bread, crusts removed
30ml (1fl oz) red wine vinegar
4 medium-size lamb fillets
1 brown onion, chopped
60g (2oz) paprika
¼ cup (60ml/2fl oz) olive oil
salt
black pepper
200g (7oz) rocket

Method

In a bowl, soak the slices of bread in the red wine vinegar and leave to one side. Place lamb fillets in a bowl and mix with onion, paprika, olive oil, salt and pepper. Place bread and rocket in a blender with a little salt and blend thoroughly. If this sauce is too strong for your liking, adjust the bread or vinegar to taste. If the sauce is too thick add a little water or a little more red wine vinegar.

Heat a barbecue or skillet until very hot. Cook lamb fillets for 5 minutes on each side; this will produce a medium-rare fillet. Cook slightly longer if a well-done fillet is preferred.

To serve place a small spoonful of rocket sauce onto plate and place the lamb fillet on top.
Serves 4

Cayenne asparagus

Savoury picnic roll

savoury picnic roll

Ingredients

Loaf

2 cups self raising flour
½ teaspoon salt
¾ cup bran
2 tablespoons butter
1 cup (250ml/9fl oz) milk

Filling

1 small onion, chopped
125g (4½oz) cheddar cheese, grated
1–2 slices bacon, chopped
1 tomato, chopped
½ capsicum, chopped
1 gherkin, chopped
salt
pepper
egg or milk, for glaze

Method

Preheat oven to 200°C (400°F).

Sift flour, salt and bran together. Rub in the butter using fingertips until mixture resembles coarse breadcrumbs. Add the milk and mix into a soft dough. Knead lightly on a floured board and roll into a rectangle, ½cm thick.

In a bowl, combine onion, cheese, bacon, tomato, capsicum, and gherkin, and season with salt and pepper to taste. Spread the mixture over the dough, leaving a 2cm (¾in) border. Roll up the dough like a swiss roll and form a horseshoe shape. Cut slits in the top of the dough at 2cm (¾in) intervals. Glaze with egg or milk and bake for 20–25 minutes.

Serve hot or cold.

seafood san choy bow

Ingredients

200g (7oz) king prawns, cooked
200g (7oz) crab meat, cooked
30ml (1fl oz) brown malt vinegar
200ml (7fl oz) olive oil
juice of 1 lemon
salt
pepper
1 large iceberg lettuce
8 slices smoked salmon
1 white onion, thinly sliced
1 avocado, thinly sliced
8 sprigs of parsley
capers, optional

Method

Peel the cooked prawns and mix with crab meat.

In a separate bowl, combine vinegar, oil, lemon and season with salt and pepper to taste. Mix well. Pour the mixture over the prawn and crab meat mixture and refrigerate. Allow to sit until ready to serve.

Carefully peel off 8 full leaves of iceberg lettuce as they must stay whole to hold the seafood mixture. Lay out lettuce leaves and evenly spread some prawn and crab mixture into each leaf. Place a slice of smoked salmon on top of each, followed by a slice of white onion and a slice of avocado. Roll up the leaves and top with a sprig of parsley.

Capers can also be added for a bit of extra tang.

Serves 8

zucchini flowers

Ingredients

1 cup self raising flour
pepper
200ml (7fl oz) water
½ small onion
6 anchovies
flour, for dusting
16 zucchini flowers
splash of oil

Method

In a bowl, mix the flour, pepper and water together to make a reasonably thick batter. In a blender, combine the onion and anchovies together and add this mixture to the batter. Mix well.

Cover the bottom of a non-stick frying pan with oil and heat. Dust the zucchini flowers with flour and lightly coat them with the batter. Fry for about 30 seconds on each side, using two forks to turn them over, or until light brown in colour.

Ask your greengrocer to save the zucchini flowers for you as they are very seasonal. If they are not available, use vegetables of your choice but be sure to par boil them first so they are not too hard.

mushroom tart

Ingredients

Pastry
1 cup plain flour
½ cup butter, softened
1 tablespoon cold water

Filling
60g (2oz) butter
splash of olive oil
500g (1lb) mushrooms, thinly sliced
1 tablespoon pink peppercorns
400ml (14fl oz) beef stock demiglaze
   (recipe page 124)
splash of white wine
1 tablespoon tomato Provençale
   (recipe page 117)
½ cup Parmesan cheese, grated
4 eggs, beaten
salt
pepper

Method

To prepare the pastry, rub the flour and butter together with fingertips until it resembles breadcrumbs. Add water and knead until the dough is well combined, then refrigerate for 30 minutes.

Preheat oven to 200°C (400°F). Roll out the dough and place into a lightly greased tin. Using a fork, prick some holes into the bottom of the pastry to stop it from puffing up. Bake for 15 minutes, or until three-quarters cooked.

To make the filling, heat the butter and olive oil in a frying pan and sauté the mushrooms and pink peppercorns for 10 minutes. Add the white wine and beef stock and simmer until the mixture reduces to a nice thick sauce. Allow to cool and add tomato Provençale, Parmesan cheese, eggs, and salt and pepper to taste. Mix well and pour into the pastry case. Bake the tart for 15 minutes or until the filling is cooked. The filling should be firm when gently pushed down

Serves 6

jamaican fish cakes

Ingredients

500g (1lb) fresh Atlantic salmon
1 cup (250ml/9fl oz) white wine
1 bay leaf
sprinkle of black peppercorns, whole
200g (7 oz) smoked salmon,
  finely chopped
1 bunch of chives, finely chopped
juice of 1 lemon
2 pinches of paprika
3 pinches of cayenne pepper
salt
200ml (7fl oz) cream
150g (5½oz) self raising flour
½ cup water
2 eggs
olive oil
1 lime, cut into wedges, to serve

Method

Place Atlantic salmon in a saucepan with the white wine, bay leaf and peppercorns and cover with water. Boil for about 6–8 minutes. Remove the salmon from liquid and allow to cool.

Mash the salmon with a fork and mix with the smoked salmon. Add the chives, lemon juice, paprika, cayenne pepper and some salt to taste and combine well. Add the cream and mix thoroughly.

To make the batter, beat flour, water and eggs together. The consistency of the batter must be thick so that it can bind the fish cakes together. Add the batter to the salmon mixture slowly, mixing well, until you have a firm mixture. Place the mixture in the fridge for 1 hour. Cooling the mixture thickens it up and makes it easier to handle.

To prepare the fish cakes, spoon 1 tablespoon of the mixture onto the grill of the hotplate on the barbecue. Flatten the mixture with a spatula and cook for 2 minutes on each side or until golden brown. The fish cakes should look and feel like a pancake.

Serve with lime wedges. If you don't have a barbecue, the fish cakes can be cooked on the stove in a non-stick pan lightly coated in oil.

Serves 4

shredded beef salad

Ingredients

1 x 300g (10½oz) porterhouse steak
1 raddiccio lettuce, finely shredded
splash of olive oil
splash of balsamic vinegar
salt
pepper

Method

Cut steak into thin strips. Heat a little olive oil in a frying pan and, when the oil is hot, cook the steak strips for about 2 minutes. Toss in raddiccio and remove from the heat immediately. Don't overcook the lettuce. Stir through a splash of balsamic vinegar. Season with salt and pepper to taste and serve immediately.

Serves 4

Aristos' Tip: Other cuts of meat such as rump, blade or round steak can also be used.

coconut crab au gratin

Ingredients

4 whole crabs, or 500g (1lb) blue
  swimmer crabmeat
100g (3½oz) butter
1 onion, finely chopped
2 tablespoons coconut, dessicated
1 tablespoon curry powder
1½ cups béchamel sauce
  (recipe page 114)

Method

In a large saucepan, heat water until boiling. Add crabs, bring water back to the boil and cook for approximately 5 minutes. Remove crabs and place in cold water to stop them cooking further. Peel crabs, place meat in a bowl and set aside the 4 shells for serving.

Melt the butter in non-stick saucepan and sauté the onions until soft. Add the coconut and sauté for a further 2 minutes. Add the curry powder and 1 cup of the béchamel sauce and mix well, then add the crab meat.

Pour the mixture into the crab shells, top with the remaining béchamel sauce and place under a grill for 3 minutes or until brown.

Serve with a sprinkling of paprika.

Serves 4

Jamaican fish cakes

Quick spinach souffle

quick spinach soufflé

Ingredients

500g (1lb) fresh spinach
1 x 375g (13oz) can cream of
  mushroom soup
2 tablespoons dried French
  onion soup mix
¾ cup (185ml/6½fl oz) mayonnaise
2 eggs, beaten
⅓ cup of Parmesan cheese, grated
salt
pepper
100g (3½ oz) bacon, finely chopped

Method

Preheat oven to 180°C (350°F).

Wash and chop spinach. Thoroughly drain and combine with mushroom soup, French onion soup mixture, mayonnaise, eggs, Parmesan and salt and pepper to taste. Pour into soufflé dishes and sprinkle tops with bacon bits and a little more Parmesan.

Bake for 30 minutes and serve immediatly.

Serves 4–6

aristos' famous chilli prawns

Ingredients

600g (1¼lb) prawns, peeled
1 small bunch of basil, finely chopped
2 red chillies, finely chopped
4 tablespoons olive oil
60ml (2fl oz) brandy
½ cup (125ml/4½fl oz) white wine
2 cups (500ml/17½fl oz) tomato
  Provençale (recipe page 117)
100g (3½oz) Australian feta cheese,
  crumbled

Method

Heat the olive oil in a frying pan over moderately high heat. Sauté prawns, basil and chillies. Add the brandy and white wine and stir well. Add the tomato Provençale sauce, combining well, and simmer for 5 minutes. Add the crumbled feta cheese and toss well.

Serve with saffron rice.

Serves 4

salmon carpaccio

Ingredients

600g (¼lb) Tasmanian salmon fillet,
  skinless and boneless
1 small white onion, finely chopped
½ cup baby capers
salt
pepper
2 large sprigs of dill, roughly chopped
juice of 1 lemon
juice of 2 limes
splash of extra-virgin olive oil
drizzle of extra-virgin olive oil, extra
  for serving

Method

Cut salmon into very thin pieces about 10cm (4in) x 4cm (½in). Place them on a baking tray and evenly sprinkle over the onion and capers and season with salt and pepper to taste.

In a small bowl, mix the dill, lemon juice, lime juice and oil and combine well. Drizzle this mixture over the fish and gently mix so that all the ingredients are blended together and evenly distributed over the fish. Cover the baking tray in plastic wrap and place in fridge for about 4 hours. After a few hours, you should notice the salmon changing colour. This is the citrus cooking the fish.

To serve, arrange the salmon slices on a plate and top with a small drizzle of oil. The salmon can be served on a bed of rocket or mixed lettuce leaves. I prefer it plain, sprinkled with large crutons.

Serves 4

aristos' prawns lemonato

This recipe is perfect for the summer as it is light, tasty and very easy to prepare. Prawns, Moreton Bay bugs or scallops can also be prepared this way as a delicious alternative.

Ingredients

300g (10½oz) prawn meat
½ cup self raising flour
100ml (3½fl oz) extra-virgin
  olive oil
1 tablespoon of fresh sage,
  finely chopped
1 tablespoon basil, finely chopped
juice of ½ a lemon
good handful of breadcrumbs

Method

Lightly dust prawns in flour. Heat oil in frying pan until hot, then add prawns and sage and sauté for 3 minutes, stirring occasionally.

When the prawns are cooked, drizzle over lemon juice, sprinkle with breadcrumbs, toss and remove from heat. Serve immediately.

Serves 2

Aristos' Tip: As an alternative, 60ml (2fl oz) of dry white wine can be used instead of lemon juice. And a little chopped red chilli can be added for extra bite.

pissaladiere

Ingredients

Dough

1½ teaspoons active dried yeast
5 tablespoons warm water
1 cup plain flour
1 egg, lightly beaten
½ teaspoon salt
1 tablespoon olive oil

Topping

¼ cup (60ml/2fl oz) olive oil
1kg (2lb) onions, finely sliced
3 cloves of garlic, crushed
1 teaspoon fresh thyme or
  rosemary, chopped
1 x 200g (7oz) can anchovy fillets
1 cup black olives, pitted
salt
pepper

Method

To make the dough, dissolve the yeast in the warm water and stir. Sift the flour into a bowl and form a well in the centre. Pour the yeast mixture into the well with the egg and salt and gradually combine until it forms a dough. Knead on a floured surface for 5 minutes until dough is smooth and elastic. Grease a bowl with oil and place the dough into the bowl and turn gently to coat the entire surface. Cover with a damp cloth and set aside in a warm place for 1 hour or until it is twice its original size.

Preheat oven to 250°C (475°F).

To make the topping, heat some of the oil over moderate heat and sauté the onions, garlic and herbs until onions are translucent. Blend together half the anchovies and in a food processor, all the olives and add to the onion mixture. Season with salt and pepper to taste.

Roll out the dough and press onto a greased pie dish or pizza pan.

Spoon the topping onto the dough, leaving a broad rim round the edge. Top with remaining anchovy fillets. Brush the uncovered rim with the remaining olive oil and bake for 20–25 minutes or until dough is crisp and brown.

Serve hot with a glass of cold beer.

Serves 6

white pilaf rice

Method 1

Ingredients

30g (1oz) butter
1 cup short grain white rice
2 cups (500ml/17½fl oz) chicken stock
salt
pepper

Method 2

Ingredients

splash of oil
½ brown onion, grated
1 cup short grain white rice
2 cups chicken stock
salt
pepper

Method 1

In a medium saucepan, combine the butter, rice and stock and season with salt and pepper to taste. Mix well and bring to the boil on high heat. Cover the pan and reduce heat. Simmer for 15 minutes or until all the liquid has been absorbed. Taste the rice and, if cooked, remove from heat and allow to sit for 5 minutes before serving. If the liquid has been absorbed and the rice is still not cooked, add a little water and cook for a few more minutes.

Method 2

Preheat oven to 200°C (400°F).

Splash a small baking tray with olive oil and add the onion. Sauté for 2 minutes, then add the rice and cook for a minute. Add the rice and stock and season with salt and pepper to taste. Combine well and cover with aluminium foil. Place in the oven and allow to cook for 15 minutes. If the rice is cooked, remove from oven and allow to sit for 5 minutes still covered. If the rice is not cooked, add water and return to the oven for a further 5 minutes or until rice is cooked.

Serves 4

Aristos' Tip: Both of these styles of rice are great served with saucy meat dishes, like osso bucco (recipe page 64).

Pissaladiere

Pumpkin pilaf

pumpkin pilaf

Ingredients

4 tablespoons olive oil
4 sprigs of rosemary, 2 finely chopped
  and 2 whole
1 garlic clove, whole
1 bay leaf
500g (1lb) Japanese pumpkin, peeled
  and chopped into small chunks
1 small brown onion, finely chopped
300g (10½oz) arborio rice
1l (1⅔pints) chicken stock (fresh,
  canned or made from stock cubes)
30g (1oz) butter
60g (2oz) Parmesan cheese, grated
salt
pepper

Method

Heat 2 tablespoons of oil in a saucepan and add the whole rosemary sprigs, garlic, bay leaf and pumpkin. Cook for 20 minutes on low heat until pumpkin softens. Remove the rosemary sprigs, garlic and bay leaf.

In another saucepan, heat remaining oil and sauté onion over medium heat until soft. Add rice and stir for a few minutes until translucent. Add a little of the stock and then the pumpkin mixture. Slowly add more stock until it is all used and absorbed by the rice, stirring from time to time to prevent the pilaf sticking to the pan.

Remove the saucepan from the heat and stir in the butter and Parmesan. Season with salt and pepper to taste. Sprinkle with the chopped rosemary.

Serves 4

prawns à la prosciutto

Ingredients

150g (5½oz) ricotta cheese
150g (5½oz) Greek feta cheese
60g (2oz) Parmesan cheese, grated
1 egg, beaten
pepper
16–20 large prawns
8 thin slices prosciutto
splash of olive oil
sprinkle of dried mint leaves

Method

In a bowl, combine the ricotta, feta, Parmesan, egg and pepper and set aside.

Peel and devein the prawns, leaving the tail on. Slit the prawn down the middle of the inside and place a small spoonful of the cheese mixture into slit, then wrap the prawn in a slice of prosciutto to seal.

Heat the oil in a frying pan and cook prawns on both sides until prosciutto is cooked.

Serves 4-6

barbecue chicken kebabs

Ingredients

6 chicken thighs, approximately 600g
  (¼lb), boned and cut into 3cm (¼in)
  squares
1 small brown onion, roughly chopped
1 teaspoon sweet paprika
sprinkle dry oregano
2 garlic cloves, roughly chopped
splash of olive oil
salt
pepper

Method

In a large mixing bowl, combine the chicken, oregano, paprika and garlic and season with salt and pepper. Add olive oil and coat well. Refrigerate for at least 24 hours to marinate.

Soak 8 bamboo sticks in cold water for 30 minutes and slide the chicken pieces onto the sticks just before you are ready to cook. Don't pack the chicken pieces too tightly together as this will cause Heat the barbecue and cook for about 5 minutes on each side.

Serves 4

Aristos' Tip: Ideally, meat should be marinated for 24 hours although I have marinated meat for up to 3 days with fantastic results. Marinating meat for at least 4 hours still gives a good result. Pork and lamb can also be used.

toni's quattro formaggio

Toni and her husband David eat at my restaurant quite regularly. Toni once cooked and delivered this lovely pasta dish to the restaurant for the boys in the kitchen and myself. We all really enjoyed it and I hope you do too.

Ingredients
500g (1lb) penne pasta, rigatoni
60g (2oz) butter
250ml (9fl oz) thickened cream
zest of 2 lemons
100g (3½oz) Parmesan cheese, grated
100g (3½oz) Gruyère cheese, grated
100g (3½oz) cheddar cheese, grated
100g (3½oz) cream cheese

Method
In a large saucepan, cook the pasta in boiling salted water until al dente. Drain well and set aside.

In a medium saucepan, melt the butter and add the cream and lemon zest. Mix well and add the Parmesan, Gruyère, cheddar and cream cheese and mix well until all the cheese has melted. Add the pasta and combine well.

Serve immediately with some chilli or truffle oil.

If you feel that the pasta is a bit thick add a touch of cream to achieve the right consistency. If it is too runny add more Parmesan to thicken.

Serves 6

medley of pizza

Ingredients
8 slices Italian continental loaf
splash of olive oil
sprinkle of oregano
200g (7oz) mozzarella cheese, grated
4 cherry tomatoes
8 anchovies
4 teaspoons ricotta cheese
4 slices prosciutto
4 whole pickled artichokes, roughly
   chopped
sprinkle of cayenne pepper or chilli
   (optional)

Method
Preheat oven to 200°C (400°F).

Using an 8cm (3in) pastry cutter, cut each slice of bread into a circle and discard the crusts. Brush one side of the bread circles with olive oil and sprinkle with oregano. Place the circles onto a baking tray oil-side down.

Place grated mozzarella on 4 of the slices of bread. Place a cherry tomato on top and cris-cross two anchovies on top of the tomato.

On the remaining bread circles, spread a spoonful of ricotta and place a slice of prosciutto on top. Evenly top with artichoke. To add a bit of a kick, sprinkle with cayenne pepper or chilli.

Put baking tray into the oven and bake for about 10 minutes or until the cheese melts. Serve hot.

Serves 4

Aristos' Tip: You can vary the toppings depending on what you have available in the fridge and pantry on the day.

prawns à la greque

Ingredients
16 large prawns, raw
3 tablespoons olive oil
2 garlic cloves, crushed
2 tomatoes, finely chopped
sprinkle of sugar
handful of feta cheese, cut into cubes
2 sprigs of parsley, chopped
salt
pepper

Method
Peel and devein prawns, leaving the tails on. Heat oil over high heat and sauté garlic for 1 minute. Add prawns, tomatoes, sugar, feta, parsley and salt and pepper to taste. Cook for 5–6 minutes or until prawns are cooked.

Serve with fresh crusty bread.

Serves 4

spinach and feta pastries

Ingredients

Pastry

500g (1lb) plain flour
pinch salt
170g (6oz) butter, soft
250ml (9fl oz) cold water

Filling

1 large brown onion, chopped
1 bunch of spring onions, chopped
1 garlic clove, finely chopped
3 tablespoons olive oil
1 bunch silverbeet, washed and
    chopped, not stalks
3 bunches English spinach, washed
    and chopped
½ teaspoon ground nutmeg
2 tablespoons dill, chopped
salt
pepper
120g (4 oz) feta cheese
olive or vegetable oil for frying,
    optional

Method

To make the pastry, sift flour and salt into a bowl. Rub the butter into the mixture with fingertips until it resembles breadcrumbs. Make a well in centre of the mixture and add water and stir with the blade of a knife. Knead slightly. Cover with a tea towel so the mixture does not dry out. Set aside.

To make the filling, in a saucepan sauté the onion, spring onions and garlic in olive oil over moderate heat. When onion is transparent gradually add chopped silverbeet and spinach. Stir nutmeg and dill through and add some salt and pepper to taste; be careful with the salt as feta cheese can be quite salty. Simmer until spinach is wilted. Turn filling mixture into a colander and strain. Leave mixture to cool. When cool, crumble feta cheese through the mixture.

Roll out pastry into 15cm (6in) circles and roll the pastry as thin as you can. Place a tablespoon of the mixture in centre the of each pastry. Fold one side of the pastry over to the other side and press the edges to make a half moon shape.

In an electric frypan, cover the bottom of the pan with oil and heat. Gently fry pastries until lightly browned. They can also be baked in an oven at 200°C (400°F) instead of frying although frying the pastry is preferable. Place on paper towel to absorb excess oil and serve when cool.

Makes 20

another filling for pastries

Ingredients

1 tablespoon butter
500g (1lb) leeks, bulbs only,
    chopped
1 small onion, chopped
500g (1lb) lamb mince
¼ teaspoon nutmeg
salt
pepper
gravy powder

Method

Heat the butter in a large saucepan and sauté the leeks and onion. Add the lamb mince and brown. Add the nutmeg and season with salt and pepper to taste. Sprinkle filling with gravy powder to thicken.

Makes 20

mains

mains

I've learnt a lot from my dad over the years, and he's still teaching me now even though he's officially retired.

These days you'll find him picking fish straight from the fishermen's boats and driving it down to the restaurant to make sure **I get the best of the catch** — and that it arrives fresh. If he's got time he'll stay on. While we're working he loves to sit in the kitchen, drinking a glass of red wine and chatting to my brother and I. Whenever a plate goes past on its way to a table, he looks it over, nods and then says to us in Greek: **"Beautiful plates!"**

Although I have a restaurant of my own, dad likes to remind me every now and then that he's been around for a long time and he's still the master — which he is!

Ralph and his father,
Vince Barbaro, in
their butcher shop.

I remember one hot day I was unloading fish out the
back of the restaurant and dad came to have a look.
"Make sure you throw a bit of extra ice on those and
stack the big fish on the bottom," he said. I already knew
that was the way to do it because he'd taught me, but I
smiled anyway, threw in some more ice and kept going.
A minute later he looked up again. "They might need a
bit of extra ice," he advised, pointing to the sun, which
was directly overhead. The fish were going straight into
the processing room and would have only been in the
back of the ute for another five minutes, but he still
wanted more ice, so I shovelled in some more. Just then
I was called away to the phone. By the time I got back
the fish had been sitting there for about 20 minutes.
He was right about the ice, but how did he know the
phone was going to ring?

garlic and sage pasta

Ingredients
2 garlic cloves, finely chopped
1 small bunch sage, finely chopped
100g (3½oz) butter
500g (1lb) No. 7 spaghetti
splash of olive oil
1 small bunch parsley, finely chopped
salt
pepper
100g (3½oz) Parmesan cheese, grated

Method
In a non-stick frying pan, sauté garlic and sage in butter. When butter has browned remove pan from heat and put to one side.

Boil pasta in a large pot of salted water with olive oil. This will ensure the pasta does not stick to the pot. Cook for about 10 minutes or until the pasta is al dente. Do not overcook the pasta. Drain pasta but do not rinse as this removes the starch. Spread pasta over a large tray to cool.

Put pan with the browned butter back on heat, add parsley and sauté for a few minutes. Add pasta and mix well. Season with salt and pepper to taste and serve while hot.

Top with Parmesan cheese and serve with a fresh green or mixed salad.
Serves 4

fettuccini carbonara à la aristos

Ingredients
500g (1lb) fettuccini
150g (5½oz) bacon, finely chopped
100g (3½oz) butter
1 small tin champignons, drained
2 eggs
100ml (3½fl oz) cream
150g (5½oz) Romano or Parmesan
    cheese, grated

Method
In a large saucepan, cook pasta in boiling salted water until al dente. Drain and set aside.

In a frying pan, sauté bacon in butter until crispy. Add champignons and the cooked pasta and mix well until heated through. Add the eggs and mix vigorously so the egg is cooked from the heat of the pasta. Slowly add cream until pasta is moist.

Serve immediately with Romano or Parmesan cheese on top.
Serves 4-6

lamb shanks

Ingredients
4 lamb shanks
2 tablespoons butter
1 tablespoon olive or vegetable oil
1 large onion, chopped
1 x 400g (14oz) can whole peeled
    tomatoes
1 cup (250ml/9fl oz) chicken stock
¼ cup (50ml/2fl oz) vermouth
½ teaspoon powdered ginger
pinch cinnamon
salt
pepper

Method
Remove any excess fat from lamb shanks.

Melt butter and oil in a heavy, flameproof casserole dish. Brown the shanks and remove from pan.

Add the onion and sauté until tender. Stir in the tomatoes, chicken stock, vermouth, ginger, cinnamon and season with salt and pepper to taste.

Return shanks to casserole dish and combine well with the sauce. Lower the heat and simmer for 2 hours or until the meat comes free from the bone.

Serve with mashed potato and peas or with rice and salad.
Serves 4

Garlic and sage pasta

Chicken parcels

chicken parcels

Ingredients

1 chicken breast
splash of olive oil
splash of white wine
salt
pepper
4 sheets filo pastry
1 tablespoon butter, melted
½ camembert cheese, thinly sliced
¼ avocado, sliced

Method

Preheat oven to 180°C (350°F). Cut the chicken into small pieces and sauté in a frying pan until three-quarters cooked. Add white wine and season with salt and plenty of pepper. Allow to cool.

Brush one side of filo pastry with some butter, lay the second layer of filo on top and repeat the process until you have 4 layers of filo on top of one another. Cut the pastry in half and place it lengthways, horizontally in front of you. Place pieces of chicken, camembert and avocado in the middle of the pasty. Fold the top over and roll into a 'bon bon' by twisting the ends.

Place on a baking tray and brush with the remaining butter. Bake for 15 minutes or until pastry is golden brown.

Serves 2

fillet steak with vegetable sauce

Ingredients

2 large celery stalks, roughly chopped
1 large brown onion, roughly chopped
2 large carrots, roughly chopped
1 large turnip, roughly chopped
1 garlic clove, roughly chopped
10 sprigs of flat-leaf parsley
1 sprig of basil
1 bay leaf
1 clove
100g (3½oz) cheap beef
1 cup (250ml/9fl oz) dry red wine
60g (2oz) butter
splash of olive oil
4 fillet steaks, 3–4cm (1-1½in) thick

Method

In a medium saucepan, place the celery, onion, carrots, turnip, garlic, parsley, basil, bay leaf and clove and mix well. Place the cheap beef on top and pour red wine over the ingredients. Combine well and place the lid on the saucepan. Cook over medium heat for 30 minutes without stirring. Then remove the lid, season with salt and pepper to taste and stir well. Cook for a further 15 minutes uncovered. Remove the saucepan from the heat and discard the beef, clove and bay leaf. Place the remaining mixture in a blender and blend until smooth.

In a non stick frying pan, heat the butter and oil and add the vegetable mixture. Simmer for about 5 minutes or until the mixture thickens.

Heat the barbecue hotplate or grill and cook the fillet steak for about 5–7 minutes on each side for a medium-rare result.

To serve, spoon the sauce over the steak and serve with crusty bread.

This vegetable sauce also goes well with veal cutlets.

Serves 4

alicia's special veal cutlets

Angie Papandopoulos is one of my best friends. He and his daughter Alicia are frequent visitors to my restaurant. Now, the restaurant specialises in seafood, and Alicia doesn't eat seafood. But one day she ate a meal of veal cutlets at my home, and ever since then her father has called up whenever they're coming into the restaurant to request Alicia's special veal cutlets.

Ingredients

1 bunch Italian parsley, finely chopped
1 x large packet of breadcrumbs
100g (3½oz) Parmesan cheese, grated
12 thin slices veal or baby beef topside
flour, for dusting
2 eggs, beaten
100ml (3½fl oz) milk
olive oil
1 cup of tomato Provençale (recipe page 117)
500g (1lb) bacon
2 x 300g (10½oz) tinned champignons, sliced
1kg (2lb) cheddar cheese, grated

Method

In a bowl, mix parsley, breadcrumbs and parmesan and set aside. Lightly dust meat in flour. In a separate bowl, mix eggs and milk and dip floured meat into mixture, then coat meat with breadcrumb mixture.

In a frying pan, heat a splash of oil and, when hot, fry meat slices for 3 minutes on each side. Once cooked pat dry with paper towel to remove any excess oil and place on baking tray. Take a spoonful of the tomato provençale and lightly spread over meat. Sprinkle the bacon, champignons and grated cheese on top. Place under the grill until cheese melts and serve immediately.
Serves 6

aristos' simple spaghetti bolognese

I've never met a bachelor who doesn't cook spaghetti bolognese – and they all think they're pretty good at it. On the basis of the few I've tasted I would say this recipe is a must!

Ingredients

1 large onion, finely chopped
2 tablespoons butter or olive oil
750g (1½lb) minced beef
250g (9oz) chicken or pork, minced
6 cups tomato Provençale
  (recipe page 117)
2 tablespoons tomato paste
1 cinnamon stick
1 bay leaf
salt
pepper
Parmesan cheese, grated

Method

In a saucepan, sauté onion in butter or olive oil. When onion is transparent add beef and chicken and cook until brown. Add Provençale sauce, tomato paste, cinnamon, bay leaf and salt and pepper to taste. Simmer for 1½ hours, stirring occasionally. (If the sauce is too thick, dissolve a chicken stock cube in 500ml water and pour in. If the sauce is too thin, allow to cook for a further 30 minutes, or until it has reached the right consistency).

Serve over freshly cooked spaghetti or fettucine with Parmesan cheese.

Serves 6

garlic spaghetti

Ingredients

200ml (7fl oz) extra-virgin olive oil
2–3 chillies, chopped
3–4 large garlic cloves, coarsely
  chopped
500g (1lb) No. 5 spaghetti
1 heaped tablespoon flatleaf parsley,
  chopped
Parmesan cheese, grated

Method

Heat oil in saucepan. Add chilli and garlic and sauté over low heat for 5–10 minutes.

In a large saucepan, cook spaghetti in boiling salted water until al dente. Drain well and add the parsley and garlic mixture to the pasta. Toss well.

Serve with Parmesan cheese.

Serves 4

baked meatballs

Ingredients

500g (1lb) beef mince
200g (7oz) chicken mince
splash of water
3 slices stale bread, crusts removed
1 cup (250ml/9fl oz) milk
2 sprigs of parsley, finely chopped
2 sprigs of mint, finely chopped
pinch of oregano, dried
1 egg, beaten
salt
pepper
2 cups (500ml/17½fl oz) tomato
  Provençale (recipe page 117)
Parmesan cheese

Method

Preheat oven to 180°C (350°F).

In a large mixing bowl, combine the beef and chicken mince with a splash of water. Soak the bread in milk and add it to the meat. Add the parsley, mint, oregano and egg and combine well. Season with salt and pepper to taste.

Grease a medium-size baking dish. Using the palms of your hands, roll a spoonful of the mixture into a ball. Place the meatball into the baking dish and continue until all the mixture has been used.

Cover the meatballs with the tomato Provençale and bake for about 15 minutes. Turn the meatballs over using two forks and continue cooking for 30 minutes or until the meatballs are cooked through.

To serve, sprinkle with Parmesan cheese and serve with mashed potatoes or white piaffi rice (recipe page 32).

Serves 4

Aristos' simple
spaghetti bolognese

Arthur's fish

arthur's fish

If there's one thing I remember about growing up in my parents' restaurant, it's that everybody ate two fried eggs with every meal. On a long weekend we would use dozens of eggs. There was one old guy, Arthur Wake, who used to work for my father washing dishes, and his favourite was crumbed snapper with 2 fried eggs, drizzled with Worcestershire sauce.

Ingredients

1kg (2lb) fish fillets, skin removed and deboned
2 eggs
150ml (5½fl oz) milk
200g (7oz) breadcrumbs
60g (2oz) Parmesan cheese, grated
1 small bunch flat-leaf parsley, finely chopped
20 capers
self raising flour, for dusting

Method

Ask your fishmonger to cut fish into four 250g (9oz), or eight 125g (4½oz) fillets. In a bowl, beat eggs and milk.

In a separate bowl mix breadcrumbs, cheese and parsley. Finely chop capers and pat dry to remove any excess liquid. Add capers to the breadcrumb mixture.

Dust fish fillets in flour, dip in egg wash and coat with the breadcrumb mixture. Coat the bottom of a frying pan with vegetable oil or olive oil. (Do not use extra-virgin olive oil as the flavour can overpower the fish.) When oil is quite hot, place fillets in pan. Cook each side, turning the fillets over with two forks rather than a spatula.

To tell if fish is cooked, gently put a fork into the thickest part of flesh. If flesh is still translucent cook a little longer. Remove from pan and drain on paper towel.

Serve with tartare sauce (Recipe page 127).

Serves 4

Aristos' Tip: If fish fillets are very thick, cut slits through thickest part. This will allow the heat to penetrate and cook the fish more evenly.

chicken paprika

Ingredients

2 medium onions, chopped
30g (1oz) plain flour
1 teaspoon paprika
1 teaspoon salt
pepper
4 chicken Marylands
30g (1oz) butter
3 teaspoons tomato paste
1 teaspoon sugar
125ml (4½fl oz) water
1 x 300ml (10½fl oz) carton sour cream
parsley, chopped

Method

In a bowl, mix the flour, paprika, salt and pepper together. Coat chicken in the seasoned flour.

Melt butter in a large frying pan and sauté the onions until transparent. Add chicken and fry until lightly browned. Stir any remaining flour seasoning into the pan, and add tomato paste, sugar and water. Cover and simmer for about 40 minutes or until the chicken is cooked through. Stir sour cream into pan. Pour into a warm serving dish and sprinkle with freshly chopped parsley.

Serve with noodles or rice and a green salad.

Serves 4

braised chicken in tomato salsa

Ingredients

1 onion, finely chopped
60g (2oz) butter
6 chicken Marylands
2 tablespoons tomato paste or
  tomato Provençale (recipe page 117)
½ cup (125ml/4½fl oz) dry white wine
½ teaspoon cinnamon
1 x 500g (1lb) packet frozen
  peas, minted
salt
pepper

Method

Preheat oven to 150°C (300°F).

In a casserole dish sauté the onion in butter until transparent. Add chicken and brown. Add tomato paste, wine, cinnamon and salt and pepper to taste. Cover casserole dish and place in oven to braise for 35 minutes. Add minted peas and cook for a further 10 minutes.

Serve with mashed potato and steamed carrots.

Serves 6

stifardo (beef & onion stew)

Ingredients

1kg (2lb) stewing steak
olive oil
1 large brown onion, chopped
2 garlic cloves, chopped
400ml (14fl oz) red wine
150ml (5½fl oz) brown malt vinegar
2 cups (500ml/17½fl oz)
  tomato Provençale (recipe page 117)
1 cinnamon stick
1 bay leaf
salt
pepper
10 brown pickling onions

Method

In a saucepan, sauté the onion and garlic in olive oil. Add the steak and cook until the meat browns. Add the wine and vinegar and leave to simmer for 15–20 minutes. Add the tomato Provençale, cinnamon stick and bay leaf and season with salt and pepper to taste. Simmer for a further 15 minutes then add the pickling onions. If the sauce is a too thick, add a cup of water to achieve the right consistency. Leave to simmer until onions are cooked through.

Serve with mashed potatoes or white piaffi rice (recipe page 32).

Serves 4-6

easy chicken cacciatore

Ingredients

12 boneless chicken thighs
4 tablespoons olive oil
½ cup (125ml/4½fl oz) white wine
or water
2 cups (500ml/17½fl oz) Janice's
  cacciatore sauce (recipe page 117)

Method

In a large saucepan, heat the oil and sauté the chicken until brown. Add the wine and the cacciatore sauce and combine well. Place the lid on the saucepan and gently simmer for 15 minutes. Remove lid and simmer for a further 20 minutes.

Serve with white piaffi rice (recipe page 32).

Serves 4

Braised chicken in
tomato salsa

Fish and potato bake

fish and potato bake

Ingredients

2 tablespoons butter
2 tablespoons flour
300ml (14fl oz) tomato juice
100ml packet of tomato soup mix
sprinkle of sugar
2 tablespoons parsley, chopped
salt
pepper
500g (1lb) potatoes
1 small onion, grated
100ml (3½fl oz) milk
1 tablespoon (20g) butter
4 x 250g (9oz) fish fillets, preferably
   snapper

Method

Preheat oven to 180°C (350°C). To make a roux, melt butter in a small saucepan. Add flour and mix to form a smooth paste. Stir in tomato juice, packet of tomato soup mix and sugar and cook until the mixture thickens. Add parsley and season with salt and pepper to taste.

To make the mash potatoes, boil potatoes until soft. Mash with a masher or in a blender. Add the onion, milk and butter and mix well.

Grease a pie dish and pour half the roux into the dish. Lay fish fillets on top and pour the rest of the roux over the fish. Top with mashed potato and bake for about 20 minutes.

Serve with rocket salad (recipe page 106).

Serves 4

roast chicken

Ingredients

1 large chicken
6 slices of stale bread, crusts removed
1 brown onion, grated
½ cup (125ml/4½fl oz) olive oil
salt
pepper
¼ cup (60g/2oz) oregano
2 cups (500ml/17½fl oz) water
1 tablespoon gravy powder

Method

Preheat oven to 220°C (425°F).

Place bread in blender and blend until crumbed. Pour crumbs into bowl and add grated onion and half the olive oil and mix well using hands. Stuff the chicken with the mixture. Rub salt and pepper over chicken and sprinkle with oregano. Place in a baking tray with two cups of water and the remaining olive oil. (You can place the chicken on a baking rack above the tray if you prefer). Cook for 15 minutes and baste. Turn chicken over onto other side and continue cooking for 50–60 minutes, basting occasionally.

To test if chicken is cooked, spear the chicken on the thickest part of the breast, if the juice is clear, the chicken is cooked; if not, keep it in the oven for another 10 minutes.

Once cooked, remove from oven, cover in foil and keep warm. Place baking tray on stove top and remove any excess oil with a spoon. Add gravy powder to pan juices and stir. You can also add some brandy and pepper for a delicious gravy.

Serves 4

Aristos' Tip: Basting the chicken with melted butter, liquid or stock while it is cooking will add flavour and colour and prevent the poultry from drying out.

garlic prawns

There are a lot of recipes for garlic prawns but I don't think any are as tasty or as easy as this one. It's a great dish for dinner parties as it takes all of about 5 minutes to make!

Ingredients
600g (1¼lb) prawns
salt
3 tablespoons olive oil
2 garlic cloves, sliced
1 small bunch of basil, finely chopped
¼ cup breadcrumbs
lemon wedges, to serve

Method
De-vein prawns then wash and sprinkle with salt. Put to one side to drain.

In a non-stick frying pan, heat oil until hot and add garlic and basil. Add prawns, turning them over continuously. Sauté for 3 minutes. Sprinkle breadcrumbs into pan until prawns are coated and all the oil absorbed.

Serve with lemon wedges.
Serves 4

italian pork chops

Ingredients

4 pork loin chops
4 tablespoons olive oil
2 garlic cloves, crushed
2 cups (500ml/17½fl oz) of tomato
    Provençale (recipe page 117)
salt
pepper
125g (4½oz) mushrooms, chopped
3 green capsicums, cut into strips
flour, for dusting

Method

Trim fat from pork chops. Flatten chops and dust with flour.

Heat two tablespoons of olive oil and fry the garlic. Add chops and fry until golden brown on both sides. Remove from pan and keep warm.

Add the tomato Provençaleto the pan juices and season with salt and pepper to taste. Stir well and simmer for 5 minutes. Add the mushrooms and simmer for a further 5 minutes. Return chops to the pan simmer for 15 minutes.

In another frying pan, sauté the capsicum strips in the remaining oil.

To serve, arrange the pork on dinner plates, drizzling the sauce over the top. Place the pepper strips on top.

Serves 6

asian style chicken drumsticks

Ingredients

juice of 1 lemon
zest of 1 lemon
2 tablespoons honey
2 tablespoons soy sauce
2 teaspoons minced garlic
2 tablespoons sweet chilli sauce
juice of 2 limes
2 tablespoons coriander leaves,
    finely chopped
olive oil or vegetable oil
8 chicken drumsticks
lemon wedges, to serve

Method

Combine lemon juice, lemon zest, honey, soy sauce, garlic, sweet chilli sauce, lime juice and coriander leaves in a bowl and mix well.

In a separate bowl, cover chicken drumsticks with the marinade and refrigerate for 2 hours.

Preheat oven to 200°C (400°F). Grease a large oven-proof baking tray with oil and place the drumsticks on the tray. Bake for 30 minutes or until the chicken is cooked.

Serve with lemon wedges.

Serves 4

grilled swordfish

Ingredients

1 slice stale bread, crusts removed
splash of red wine vinegar
salt
pepper
splash of olive oil
6 anchovies
12 kalamata olives, pitted
12 capers
4 x 300g (10½oz) swordfish steaks
juice of 2 lemons

Method

Splash the bread with red wine vinegar and season with salt and pepper to taste. Set aside.

In a blender, mix the oil, anchovies, olives and capers. Add bread and blend until smooth. Set aside.

Heat the barbecue and place the fish on the hottest part and cook for about 2–3 minuntes on each side for a medium rare fish. Allow a few more minutes on each side if you prefer the fish well-done.

Serve immediately on a bed of rocket or on its own. Spoon a small amount of the anchovy and olive mixture into the middle of the fish and drizzle with lemon juice

Serves 4

Italian pork chops

Lamb casserole with
feta dumplings

lamb casserole with feta dumplings

Ingredients

1kg (2lb) lamb, diced
1 tablespoon olive oil
2 large onions, chopped
2 garlic cloves
2 x 400g (14oz) tins of whole tomatoes
1 cup tomato paste
¼ cup (50ml/2fl oz) red wine
fresh oregano, chopped
½ cup (125ml/4½fl oz) chicken stock
1¼ cups (300g/10½oz) self raising flour
30g (1oz) butter, chopped
⅓ cup (80ml/3fl oz) sour cream
⅔ cup (165ml/6fl oz) milk
150g (5½oz) feta, chopped
1 tablespoon fresh oregano, chopped, extra

Method

Preheat oven to 180°C (350°F). Brown meat in olive oil, then sauté onion and garlic until transparent. Add tomatoes, tomato paste, red wine, oregano and stock and bring to the boil. Transfer into a casserole dish and bake for about 1½ hours or until lamb is tender.

To make dumplings, mix flour, butter, sour cream, milk, feta and extra oregano in a bowl and combine well. Drop heaped tablespoons of the dumpling mixture onto the surface of the hot lamb casserole and bake for a further 25 minutes or until dumplings are puffed and brown.

Serves 4

roast lamb cutlets (lemonato)

Ingredients

salt
pepper
30g (1oz) oregano
100ml (3½fl oz) olive oil
8 lamb cutlets, thick
3 large potatoes, cut into small wedges
juice of 1 lemon

Method

Preheat oven to 200°C (400°F). Rub salt, pepper, half the oregano and half the olive oil on the lamb cutlets and place in a baking dish. Cover the bottom of baking dish with water and the remainder of the oil. Bake for about 15 minutes, turning when necessary. Remove from oven, add potatoes and return to the oven until lamb is almost done, about 15–20 minutes. When the meal is almost ready, remove from oven, sprinkle with remaining oregano and lemon juice and continue cooking until done.

Serves 4

lasagna

Ingredients

1kg (2lb) beef mince
1 brown onion, chopped
2 garlic cloves, chopped
olive oil
4 cups (1¾ pints) tomato
  Provençale (recipe page 117)
2 tablespoons tomato paste
2 bay leaves
1 cinnamon stick
2 chicken stock cubes
12 lasagna sheets
Parmesan cheese, grated
mozzarella cheese, thinly sliced
ham, thinly sliced and cut into squares
1 egg, boiled and roughly chopped
2 cups (500ml/17½fl oz) béchamel
  sauce (recipe page 114)

Method

In a large saucepan, sauté the beef, onion and garlic until brown. Add the tomato Provençale, then the tomato paste, bay leaves and cinnamon stick and season with salt and pepper to taste. Combine well. Add 1 cup (250ml/9fl oz) of water and the crumbled stock cubes. Simmer together for 1½ hours, stirring occasionally. The sauce needs to be thick, so adjust the water and stock until you have the right consistency.

In a saucepan, cook 12 lasagna sheets in boiling salted water. When they are three-quarters cooked, drain and place in a bowl of iced water to stop the cooking process. Lay sheets on tea towels and pat dry.

Preheat oven to 180°C (350°F). In a 30cm (12in) x 25cm (10in) baking tray place enough pasta sheets to cover the bottom of the tray (try not to overlap). Pour some sauce over pasta sheets, then sprinkle over some Parmesan cheese, mozzarella, ham and boiled egg. Cover with pasta sheets and repeat this process until the tray is full and finish with pasta sheets on top. Top with béchamel sauce and bake in oven for about 30 minutes or until golden brown.

Serves 6

farfalle with smoked salmon and snow peas

Ingredients

500g (1lb) farfalle pasta
4 whole spring onions, chopped
60g (2oz) capers
100g (3½oz) snow peas, chopped
splash of olive oil
30g (1oz) butter
250g (7oz) fresh Tasmanian smoked
  salmon
1 cup (250ml/9fl oz) dry white wine
50ml (2fl oz) of cream
Parmesan cheese
salt
pepper

Method

Place pasta in a large pot of boiling salted water with olive oil. (This will ensure the pasta does not stick to the pot). Cook for about 10 minutes, stirring regularly, or until the pasta is al dente. Do not overcook the pasta. Drain and set aside.

In a saucepan, sauté spring onions, capers and snow peas in butter and olive oil. Add smoked salmon, white wine and cream and simmer for 5 minutes. Add cooked pasta, and Parmesan and season with salt and pepper to taste. Combine well and serve.

Serves 4

Aristos' Tip: You can also add a spoonful of black or red caviar to this recipe.

Lasagna

Osso bucco

osso bucco

Ingredients

2 veal shanks, cut into 2cm (¾in) slices
self raising flour, for dusting
splash of olive oil
1 onion, sliced
1 carrot, sliced
1 garlic clove, crushed
2 bay leaves
2 sprigs parsley, chopped
lemon zest, grated, to taste
1 cup (250ml/9fl oz) water
3 tablespoons tomato paste
1 cup (250ml/9fl oz) red wine
salt
pepper

Method

Dust the shank pieces in flour, shaking off the excess. Cover the bottom of frying pan with oil. When oil is hot, fry shanks until brown on both sides. Transfer the meat to another saucepan and set aside.

In the same frying pan used to brown the shanks, sauté the onion, carrot and garlic. Tip it all into the saucepan with the veal and add the bay leaves, parsley, lemon zest, water, tomato paste and red wine. (A spoonful of tinned tomato soup may be added at this stage to lend sweetness if desired). Season with salt and pepper. Simmer for about 1 hour.

Serve with fettucine or mashed potato.

Serves 4

butter bean pasta

Ingredients

500g (1lb) spaghetti No 7
1 brown onion, chopped
1 garlic clove, chopped
100g (3½oz) bacon, chopped
4 tablespoons olive oil
1 x 375ml (13oz) tinned butter beans
small bunch parsley, finely chopped
½ cup (125ml/4½fl oz) chicken stock
2 tablespoons red wine vinegar
Parmesan cheese, grated

Method

In a large saucepan, cook spaghetti in boiling salted water until al dente. Drain and set aside.

Sauté onion, garlic and bacon in oil for a few minutes. Add beans, parsley, chicken stock and red wine vinegar. Simmer for 5 minutes and add the freshly cooked pasta.

Serve with Parmesan cheese.

Serves 4-6

papou's garlic rump

'Papou' is the Greek word for grandfather. My papou was a great cook and taught me a lot about being prepared in the kitchen and not rushing. When he cooked, the kitchen was spotless and all his ingredients were placed in regimented style. He was so precise that everyone could tell who had sliced the meat just by looking at the tray. All the slices were exactly the same thickness. This was one of his favourite recipes.

Ingredients

4 x 300g (10½oz) rump steak fillets
salt
pepper
4 garlic cloves, sliced in half lengthways
1 cup (250ml/9fl oz) dry red wine
sprinkle of oregano
splash of extra-virgin olive oil

Method

Season the rump slices with salt and pepper and place them on a medium-size baking tray. Sprinkle the garlic and oregano over the top and add the wine and a splash of olive oil. Refrigerate for 1 hour and turn the meat over to ensure the flavours go right through the meat. Refrigerate for another hour.

Using a barbecue or non-stick frying pan, cook the meat. The longer you leave the meat in the marinade, the less time you will need to cook it as the wine cures the meat.

Serve with mash potato or white piaffi rice (recipe page 32).

Serves 4

pizza

Ingredients

Dough

1 tablespoon dry yeast
½ cup (125ml/4½fl oz) warm water
500g (1lb) plain flour
½ tablespoon salt
water, as needed

Topping

150ml (5½fl oz) tomato Provençale
  (recipe page 117)
1 cup mozzarella, grated
1 cup cheddar, grated
100g (3½oz) leg ham, sliced
100g (3½oz) Hungarian salami, thinly
  sliced
60g (2oz) capsicum, roasted
¾ cup kalamata olives
60g (2oz) feta cheese, crumbled

Method

To make the dough, dissolve yeast in half a cup of luke-warm water. Place flour on a clean working bench and make a well. Tip dissolved yeast into centre of well and start to knead. Gradually add the water until the mixture becomes a nice firm dough. Knead for 10 minutes and place in a bowl covered with a damp tea towel. Set aside in a warm place until the mixture doubles in size.

Once the dough has risen, take enough dough to roll out and cover a pizza pan. Use a rolling pin if a thin crust is desired or your hands if you prefer a thick crust. Grease pizza pan with olive oil and sprinkle with flour, then place the base in the pan.

Preheat oven to 180°C (350°F). To top the pizza, spread tomato Provençale over the base using the bottom of a spoon. In a separate bowl, combine mozzarella and cheddar cheese and mix well. Lightly cover the pizza base with half the cheese. Sprinkle the ham, salami, capsicum and olives on the base so they are evenly distributed. Mix the feta with the remaining cheese and sprinkle over the pizza base.

Bake for about 1 hour or until the dough is cooked and the top is golden brown.

Serves 4-6

chicken casserole with penne pasta

Ingredients

2 onions, finely chopped
1 garlic clove, crushed
1 tablespoon butter
1 tablespoon olive oil
8–10 chicken drumsticks
1 x 420g (15oz) tin whole tomatoes
2 tablespoons tomato paste
1 teaspoon basil leaves, dried
½ cup (125ml/4½fl oz) white wine
½ cup (125ml/4½fl oz) water
½ teaspoon cinnamon
2 bay leaves
salt
pepper
500g (1lb) penne pasta
Parmesan cheese, grated

Method

Preheat oven to 180°C (350°F).

In a saucepan, sauté onion and garlic in butter and oil and cook until transparent. Add chicken drumsticks and brown. Add tomatoes, tomato paste, basil, wine, water, cinnamon, bay leaves and salt and pepper to taste. Simmer for 30 minutes. Remove saucepan from stove and pour the chicken and sauce into casserole or baking dish. Add the pasta and stir through.

Place in oven and bake for 15–20 minutes or until pasta is cooked. Remove from oven and sprinkle with salt, pepper and Parmesan cheese.

Serves 4

risotto aristos style

risotto aristos' style

Ingredients

150g (5½oz) bacon or prosciutto, finely chopped into cubes

60ml (2fl oz) extra-virgin olive oil

1 large red onion, peeled and coarsely chopped

2½ cups (625ml/1 pint) tomato Provençale (recipe page 117)

2 cups arborio rice

3 cups (750ml/1¼ pints) chicken stock, fresh or made from stock cubes

salt

pepper

6 tablespoons Pecorino or Romano cheese, grated

Method

Place a heavy-based medium-size terracotta casserole dish over medium heat and heat the oil. Add the bacon and sauté in oil for 10 minutes or until crisp. Remove from the dish and set aside.

Using the same oil, sauté the onion for about 5 minutes or until translucent. Add the tomato Provençale and simmer for 15 minutes, stirring occasionally with a wooden spoon. Remove half the tomato sauce and reserve in a bowl. Add the rice to the casserole dish and stir very well for about 4 minutes. Add half a cup of the hot stock (125ml/4½fl oz) at a time, constantly mixing with a wooden spoon. Do not add more until original stock has been completely absorbed by the rice. Just before adding the last half cup of stock, add the reserved tomato sauce. When the rice has absorbed all the liquid, season with salt and pepper to taste. At this stage, the rice should be cooked but still retain a 'bite'.

Add the bacon, mix well, and transfer to a large warm serving dish. Serve immediately with the Pecorino or Romano cheese sprinkled over the top, or stirred through the rice if desired.

Serves 4

sweet and sour pork

Ingredients

6 pork chops

flour, for dusting

½ teaspoon mustard powder

salt

pepper

1 tablespoon butter, extra

1 onion, chopped

1 green capsicum, chopped

1 tin pineapple pieces

¼ cup brown sugar

⅓ cup (35ml/1½fl oz) vinegar

1 cup (250ml/9oz) tomato sauce

1 teaspoon black sauce

Method

Remove excess fat from chops.

In a bowl, combine flour, mustard powder, salt and pepper. Lightly dust the chops in this mixture. Heat the butter in a saucepan and fry the chops until brown. Place the chops in casserole dish.

Preheat oven to 180°C (350°F). In a saucepan, cook the onion and capsicum in butter for a few minutes. Stir in the pineapple, sugar, vinegar, tomato sauce and black sauce. Heat and mix well. Pour mixture over the chops in the casserole dish and bake for 1 hour.

Serve with rice.

Serves 4

roast leg of lamb

Lamb is a staple of traditional Greek cooking, and most Greeks pride themselves on being able to cook a wonderful roast lamb. I'm no exception!

Ingredients

1 small leg of lamb, approximately
   1½kg (3lb)
3 garlic cloves
¼ cup dried oregano
salt
pepper
250ml (9fl oz) olive oil
250ml (9fl oz) water

Method

Preheat oven to 200°C (400°F).

Cut approximately five small incisions into the leg of lamb.

In a bowl, mix together garlic, oregano, salt and pepper. Mix well and fill the incisions with about half the mixture. Drizzle half the olive oil over the lamb and rub in the remainder of the garlic mixture over the outside of the meat.

Place the lamb in a baking dish and add the water and the remaining oil. Roast for about 1 hour or until cooked.

Serves 4-6

Aristos' Tip: Place cloves of garlic in a bowl of hot water for 15 minutes to allow easy removal of the skin. Ask your butcher to remove the bone from the lamb to make carving easy.

seafood gnocchi

Ingredients
1l (1½ pints) milk
1 cup semolina
1 teaspoon nutmeg
salt
pepper
200g (7oz) prawn meat, minced
2 egg yolks
60g (2oz) Parmesan cheese, grated
2 tablespoons parsley, chopped

Method
In a saucepan, bring the milk to the boil. Sprinkle in the semolina, mixing well with a whisk to avoid lumps. Add nutmeg and season with salt and pepper to taste. Cook gently for 6–8 minutes, stirring continuously. Add the prawn meat, egg yolks, Parmesan and parsley and mix well. Place mixture into a piping bag with a flat nozzle and squeeze out 4cm (1½in) long pieces. Allow to cool.

Cook gnocchi in plenty of salted boiling water for 5 minutes and drain.

Serve with a cream or tomato based sauce. Seafood gnocchi is also great with fresh basil and home-made tomato sauce (recipe page 124).
Serves 4-6

veal scallopine marsala

Ingredients
500g (1lb) veal,(or baby beef) cut into
    12 thin pieces
flour, for dusting
salt
pepper
1 tablespoon butter
3 tablespoons olive oil
1 garlic clove, chopped
180ml (6fl oz) marsala

Method
Season veal with salt and pepper and dust with flour. Melt butter and oil in large frying pan. When hot, add garlic and veal pieces and cook until brown. Remove and discard garlic when it turns brown.

When meat has browned, pour in marsala and cook over high heat for about a minute or until the sauce thickens.

Serve with mashed potatoes or garlic spaghetti (recipe page 48).
Serves 6

Aristos' Tip: As the scallopine will not easily fit into one pan, split them into 3 batches and fry separately, using a third of the marsala each time. Keep the cooked pieces warm in a low oven until all are done. If you don't like marsala, use white wine to make a delicious scallopine bianco.

lamb souvlaki

Ingredients
600g (1¼lb) diced lamb or 6 lamb
fillets, diced
sprinkle of dry oregano
1 teaspoon sweet paprika
2 garlic cloves, roughly chopped
sprinkle of cinnamon
sprinkle of nutmeg
1 sprig fresh rosemary
salt
pepper
splash of olive oil
8 medium-size pita breads
½ iceberg lettuce, shredded
3 tomatoes, sliced
1 white onion, finely sliced

Method
In a large mixing bowl, combine the lamb, oregano, paprika, garlic, cinnamon, nutmeg and rosemary and season with salt and pepper to taste. Add olive oil and coat well. Refrigerate for at least 24 hours to marinate.

Soak 8 bamboo sticks in cold water for 30 minutes and slide the lamb pieces onto the sticks just before cooking. Don't pack the lamb pieces too tightly together as this will cause the meat to cook unevenly. Heat the barbecue and cook lamb for about 5 minutes on each side or until the meat in cooked through.

Heat the pita bread on the barbecue.

To serve, place the bread on a large piece of grease-proof paper or aluminium foil. Remove the lamb pieces from the bamboo stocks and place on the bread. Place shredded lettuce, tomato and onion on top of the meat. Using the paper or foil, roll the bread up.

This is a great idea for barbecues as everyone can make their own!
Serves 4

Seafood gnocchi

spicy lamb curry

Ingredients

1kg (2lb) lamb or mutton
2 onions, finely chopped
2 tablespoons oil
1 bay leaf
1 teaspoon cinnamon, ground
1 teaspoon coriander, ground
1 teaspoon cumin, ground
2 garlic cloves, crushed
4 teaspoons curry powder
pepper
2 tablespoons flour
500g (1lb) tomatoes, skinned and
   chopped
6 teaspoons fruit chutney
1 cup (250ml/9fl oz) meat stock
1 teaspoon sugar
½ cup dried apricots
salt

Method

Trim fat from lamb. Cut lamb into bite-size pieces.

In a saucepan, sauté onions in oil until transparent and add the bay leaf, cinnamon, coriander, cumin, garlic and curry powder and combine well. Mix in the flour and simmer for a few minutes, stirring continuously. Add meat and brown lightly. Add the tomatoes, fruit chutney, meat stock, sugar and dried apricots and mix well. Season with salt and pepper to taste. Transfer the curry to a large casserole dish and cover.

Bake in a 150°C (300°F) oven for 1½ hours or simmer on top of the stove for 1 hour.

Serve with freshly steamed rice and coriander and mint chutney (recipe page 120).

Serves 4-6

Summer vegetable
frittata

summer vegetable frittata

Ingredients
250g (9oz) spaghetti
200g (7oz) zucchini, sliced
150g (5½oz) mushrooms, sliced
200g (7oz) leek, finely sliced
200g (7oz) broccoli florets
8 eggs, lightly beaten
1 tablespoon mint
100g (3½oz) peas, frozen
30g (1oz) butter
30g (1oz) Romano cheese, grated
salt
pepper

Method
In a saucepan, cook the spaghetti in boiling salted water until al dente. Drain and set aside. Preheat oven to180°C (350°F).

In a saucepan, steam or boil the vegetables in lightly salted water until tender but still firm. Drain and mix the vegetables with the eggs, mint, cheese and season with salt and pepper to taste. Lightly grease a pie dish and place spaghetti in it evenly. Pour the vegetable and egg mixture over the top to cover the spaghetti.

Bake for 20 minutes.

Serves 4-6

pasta with gravy beef sauce

Ingredients
2 tablespoons butter or olive oil
1 large onion, chopped
1 garlic clove, crushed
1kg (2lb) gravy beef, cut in chunks
3 tablespoons tinned tomato soup
1 x 420g (14oz) tin whole peeled
   tomatoes
2 bay leaves
1½ teaspoons dried basil leaves
1 teaspoon dried oregano
sprinkle of cinnamon
1 packet No. 13 Bavette spaghetti
Parmesan cheese, grated

Method
In a heavy-based saucepan, heat butter or oil and sauté onion and garlic. Add the gravy beef and brown. Add the tomato soup, tomatoes, bay leaves, basil, oregano and cinnamon and mix well. Simmer for about 1½ hours or until beef is cooked.

In a large pot, cook the pasta in boiling salted water until al dente. Drain and place in a warm dish and cover with sauce.

Serve with lots of Parmesan cheese.

Serves 4

pink snapper à la victor

Ingredients
4 x 300g (10½oz) boneless pink
   snapper fillets
2 tablespoons olive oil
salt
pepper
½ cup (125ml/4½fl oz)dry white wine
2 cups (500ml/17½fl oz) Janice's
   cacciatore sauce (recipe page 117)

Method
Preheat oven to 180°C (350°F).

Place the fish fillets in a medium-size baking dish and drizzle the oil over the fillets. Season to taste with salt and pepper. Cover the fish fillets with white wine and the cacciatore sauce. Cook in the oven for about 40 minutes or until the fish is cooked through.

Transfer fish to a warm plate and set aside. Place the sauce in a small saucepan and reduce.

Pour the sauce over the fish fillets and serve with jacket potatoes and a green salad.

Serves 4

veal caprici

Ingredients

1kg (2lb) veal, thickly sliced
2 tablespoons butter
2 tablespoons olive oil
3 slices bacon, chopped
¾ cup (185ml/6½fl oz) chicken stock
¾ cup (185ml/6½fl oz) dry white wine
sour cream
1 tablespoon capers, chopped
flour, for dusting
salt
pepper

Method

Cut meat into bite-size pieces and dust in flour seasoned with salt and pepper. In a saucepan, sauté in butter and oil until golden brown.

In a separate pan, sauté bacon and brown. Add to the veal and then add the chicken stock and wine. Cover the saucepan and cook gently for 20–25 minutes. Add sour cream and capers, mixing well. Return to low heat for 5 minutes or until cooked.

1 cup of sliced mushrooms may be added at the same time as the wine if desired.

Serve with jacket potatoes or rice, and fresh, crusty bread.
Serves 6

mum's pan fried jewfish with lemon

My dad is a great cook but even he admits that no-one can cook fish like mum! The first thing I learnt from mum is that you always use self raising flour when cooking seafood as any other flour can cause your fish to go gluggy.

Ingredients

4 x 250g (9oz) Western Australian
  jewfish fillets
salt
splash of oil
self raising flour, for dusting
juice of 2 lemons

Method

Sprinkle the fish fillets with salt and refrigerate until ready to use.

In an electric frying pan, heat the oil. Lightly dust the fish with flour and gently place in the pan to cook. Cook the fillets for about 3–4 minutes each side or until fish is cooked. To check if the fish is cooked, prick the thickest part of the fish with a fork and check that the flesh is opaque.

Drizzle the lemon juice over the fish fillets in the pan and serve immediately with iceberg and fennel salad (recipe page 109) or the boys tomato salad (recipe page 100).
Serves 4

Veal caprici

Panfried calamari

pan fried calamari

Ingredients

600g (1¼lb) squid, cleaned and sliced
  2cm (¾in) thick
self raising flour, for dusting
splash of olive oil
juice of 2 small lemons
salt

Method

Dust calamari in flour, shaking off any excess. Cover the bottom of non-stick pan with olive oil and allow to heat until oil starts to smoke. Gently place calamari into frying pan, being careful not to splash the hot oil. Cook for 6–12 minutes, turning frequently, or until golden brown and crispy.

Once cooked, drain excess oil from pan and squeeze the lemon juice over squid. Sprinkle with salt.

Serve immediately.

Serves 4

Aristos' Tip: The calamari is much easier to cook using an electric frying pan. I don't recommend using white squid tubes, which can be tough and tasteless.

glazed pork loin in aunty val's marinade

Aunty Val is the tastiest cook in the family. The only problem is that she and uncle Chris live in Honolulu so we don't get to eat her tasty treats very often.

Ingredients

12 sage leaves
salt
pepper
splash of olive oil, extra for frying
6 small shallots
16 dried apricots, roughly chopped
2 tablespoons brown sugar
2 tablespoons soy sauce
½ cup (125ml/4½ fl oz) apple cider
½ cup (125ml/4½ fl oz) water
1 whole pork loin strip, small amount
  of fat removed

Method

In a mortar and pessel, grind together the sage, salt, pepper and a splash of oil until well combined. If you don't have a mortar and pessel, use a small bowl and the back of a large spoon as the sage leaves need to be bruised to release their aromatic flavours.

Heat the oil in a medium-size saucepan and add the shallots. Sauté for about 3 minutes or until golden brown. Add the sage mixture, apricots, sugar, soy sauce, cider and water and bring to the boil. Reduce heat and simmer for about 25 minutes or until the glaze is thick and glossy. Allow to cool.

Rub half the glaze onto the pork loin and refrigerate for about 4 hours to allow the flavours to infuse the meat.

Preheat the oven to 200°C (400°F) and remove the pork loin from the refrigerator. Allow to stand at room temperature for 30 minutes. Cook the meat for about 1 hour or until the meat is cooked through.

Serve the pork loin with roasted potatoes and the remainder of the glaze.

Serves 4

Aristos' Tip: You can also use pork chops instead of a pork loin in this recipe. Instead of roasting them just cook them on the barbecue.

roast baby goat

Ingredients

1 x 3kg (6lb) side baby goat
2 garlic cloves, crushed
30g (1oz) oregano
100ml (3½fl oz) olive oil
salt
pepper
200g (7oz) butter, melted
2 brown onions, roughly chopped
1 cup (250ml/9fl oz) water
3 large ripe tomatoes, finely chopped
3 large potatoes or 10 baby potatoes
   cut into halves

Method

Ask your butcher to cut the goat side into thick pieces, leaving out the belly and rib cage.

Preheat oven to 180°C (350°F). In a bowl, mix garlic, oregano, olive oil and salt and pepper to taste. Combine well and rub over the meat.

Place the butter and onion on the bottom of a baking dish. Place meat on top and cover the bottom of dish with water. Put two-thirds of the chopped tomatoes over the top of the meat and place in oven to cook for about 1½ hours.

Add the potatoes and the remaining tomato and return to the oven for another 40 minutes or until the meat and potatoes are cooked.

Serves 4

lamb chops – george's way

My dad George loves simple food, and he loves to use good-quality ingredients, which is where my cooking style comes from. So when you are preparing food, always use the best ingredients available. As my Dad says, "there's no substitute for quality."

Ingredients

12 lamb loin chops
salt
pepper
sprinkle oregano
splash of olive oil
juice of 2 lemons

Method

Season the lamb with salt and pepper to taste. Sprinkle with oregano and a splash of olive oil. Using a grill, frying pan or barbecue hotplate, cook the lamb over high heat for about 4 minutes on each side or until cooked to your liking.

Remove the lamb from heat and drizzle the lemon juice over the chops. Serve with boiled spinach and runner beans dressed in olive oil and lemon.

Serves 4

Roast baby goat

vegetables

When it comes to cooking fresh vegetables, the less you do the better.

vegetables

I love a trip to the market! There's always something new, something you hadn't thought was in season or some surprise. It's also one of the most important places for a chef because the choices you make there can mean the difference between a great meal and an average meal. Make sure you take a close look at what you're buying and pick good-looking, fresh food.

When cooking vegetables, it's really a case of the less you do the better. All vegetables have their own unique flavours and it's really just boredom that makes people try different dishes when really **the basic ones are still the best.**

If chefs get sick of cooking something the same way, they can sometimes be tempted to suddenly try

something new, like adding roasted hazelnuts to the beans. But really, why bother? Just boil them or steam them — make sure you don't overcook them — and then drizzle over olive oil and a little lemon juice. It's one of the easiest ways to prepare vegetables, but it's still the best. They'll taste fantastic.

Don't forget the classics either. A dish like cauliflower cheese is a great example. Most people love cauliflower cheese, but if you've got the boss coming over for dinner it's probably the last thing you'd think of cooking. And that's a mistake, because if you cook it properly, it's bloody good!

aristos' vegetables

I normally prepare most vegies with olive oil and lemon juice. This method was passed down to me. We would boil or steam our vegetables and simply dress them with a little olive oil and lemon juice. Almost all vegetables, with one or two exceptions, can be served like this. Try your vegies this way and you may just be impressed with the taste!

Asparagus

Hold each asparagus spear at either end and bend until it snaps; discard woody part. Cook in boiling water for 2 minutes. Drain and drizzle with olive oil and lemon juice.

Spinach

Wash thoroughly under cold water. Bring a pan of water to the boil and add spinach. Cook for approximately 3 minutes. Do not overcook as spinach should stay a little crunchy. Drain and drizzle with olive oil and lemon juice.

Cauliflower, minted peas and onion

Place cauliflower and thinly sliced onion in a pan of boiling water until cauliflower is just cooked. Remove cauliflower from pot. Leave onion in water and add peas and a sprig of mint. cook until peas are tender. Drain, add to cauliflower, and serve with olive oil and lemon juice.

Stringless beans

Cook in boiling water or steam until tender. Drain and serve with olive oil and lemon juice.

Broccoli and cauliflower

Steam or boil until just tender. Drain well. Splash with olive oil and lemon juice.

bachelor's roast vegetables

Ingredients

any vegetables you have in the fridge
  – and I mean any vegetables!
water
olive oil
salt
pepper
dried oregano

Method

Preheat oven to 200°C (400°F).

Chop up vegetables and spread out in a baking dish. Sprinkle with water and drizzle with olive oil. Season with salt, pepper and oregano to taste. Bake for 20 minutes or until vegetables are soft.

George's lathera

Chinese greens

chinese greens

Ingredients

1 bunch of bok choy or other Chinese
  greens
1 garlic clove, finely chopped
1 teaspoon fresh ginger, finely
  chopped
2 teaspoons sesame seeds
3 tablespoons soy sauce

Method

Steam bok choy. In a bowl, combine garlic, ginger, sesame
seeds and soy sauce. Drizzle over bok choy.
Serves 2

Aristos Tip: As an optional extra you may like to add some
finely sliced fresh chilli.

george's lathera (mixed vegies)

Ingredients

1kg (2lb) green beans, French or string
3 tablespoons olive oil
1 large onion, chopped
1x 400g (14oz) tin whole peeled
  tomatoes
1 sprig of mint
pinch of sugar
salt
pepper
2 potatoes, washed and quartered
2 carrots, thickly sliced

Method

Wash and trim beans and snap them into halves. Set aside.
   Heat olive oil in a large saucepan and sauté the onion until
transparent. Add tomatoes, mint and sugar and season with
salt and pepper to taste. Simmer for 10 minutes and add the
beans, potatoes and carrots. Cover the saucepan and cook
slowly for about 30 minutes or until the beans are tender.
Serves 4-6

Aristos Tip: Vegies cooked this way can be served as an
accompaniment to meat, chicken or fish dishes alike.

rosemary potatoes

Ingredients
splash of olive oil
12 baby potatoes, peeled and halved
1 large sprig of rosemary, leaves only
2 chicken stock cubes
1 cup (250ml/9fl oz) warm water

Method
Preheat oven to 200°C (400°F).

Cover the bottom of a non-stick frying pan with oil and heat. Add potatoes and rosemary and sauté until brown. Crumble stock cubes into water and stir until dissolved.

Transfer potatoes to a baking tray and drizzle stock over the potatoes. Bake for 25 minutes or until cooked through and golden brown.
Serves 4

Aristos' Tip: Peeled potatoes should be placed in a bowl of water until ready to use to prevent them from discolouring.

crumbed eggplant

Ingredients

1 eggplant
salt
1 egg, beaten
100ml (3½fl oz) milk
60g (2oz) Parmesan cheese, grated
200g (7oz) breadcrumbs
1 small bunch of flat-leaf parsley,
   chopped
flour, for dusting
vegetable oil

Method

Cut eggplant into 2cm (¾in) thick rings and sprinkle with salt. Allow to stand for 15 minutes.

In a bowl, mix egg and milk together. In a separate bowl, mix cheese, breadcrumbs and parsley.

Remove any liquid from eggplant by patting dry with some paper towel. Dust the eggplant in flour, dip in egg wash and then coat with breadcrumb mixture.

Coat the bottom of a frying pan with vegetable oil and heat. Gently fry eggplant until cooked. Remove from pan and drain on paper towel to remove excess oil.

Serves 4

vegie fry

Ingredients

2 eggplants
salt, for eggplants
2 medium zucchini
flour, for dusting
½ cup (125ml/4½fl oz) olive oil
3 tomatoes, thickly sliced
salt
pepper

Method

Wash eggplants and slice lengthwise about 1cm (½in) thick. Sprinkle with salt and allow to stand for 20 minutes, then pat dry.

Wash zucchini, cut in half and slice each half lengthwise. Lightly dust eggplant and zucchini in flour. Heat some oil in electric frying pan at 180°C (350°F) and fry vegies until lightly browned on both sides. Remove from pan and drain on paper towel.

Arrange on platter and top with sliced tomatoes. Sprinkle with salt and pepper to taste. Serve with barbecued meat. You can also substitute the tomato for capsicum and grill the vegetables on top of the barbecue as a variation.

Serves 4-6

crumbed eggplant

salads

salads

I've got to confess I was never much of a salad eater until I started getting older and my partner raised the idea of including a few fresh veggies in my diet. Although there are a lot of different salads out there, from Caesar to Rocket and everything in between, I prefer them plain and simple.

For me, the best salads consist of a few fresh elements, with a little dressing drizzled over at the last minute to keep things crunchy. I reckon that's the way to go, and I'm not alone.

At my restaurant there's one group of guys who come in all the time. **I call them the Rat Pack.** They're all about 50 to 55 years old; they've been around and they know what they like. They come in as a group and stay for a

Many of our customers like their salads plain and simple – so do I.

few hours, trying whatever I recommend or choosing something from the menu. But there's one thing they like to have made in a very specific way: the salad.

"Mate," they say, "we just want a plain salad." "Lettuce with sliced tomato and onion and some brown vinegar on the side." They won't even let me jazz it up with a different kind of lettuce! **"We want 'real' lettuce,"** they tell me, and they mean plain, old-fashioned iceberg lettuce. No cos, no butter lettuce, just "real" lettuce.

Sometimes the basics are best.

the boys' tomato and onion salad

The "boys" are a group of great guys that dine in my restaurant on a regular basis. They are all between 50 and 60 years old, and they always ask for this salad as it reminds them of when they were young.

Ingredients

3 ripe Roma tomatoes, cut into thick
  slices
1 white onion, finely sliced
pepper
drizzle of olive oil
splash of brown malt vinegar
12 pieces semi-matured cheddar
  cheese, thinly sliced

Method

Place a layer of tomatoes in a serving dish and layer the onion slices on top. You can use one layer of tomato and onion for this dish or several alternate layers depending on the size of your dish.

Sprinkle the top with salt and pepper to taste and drizzle olive oil. Add a splash of vinegar. Use a potato peeler to shave off 12 pieces of cheese and place these on top of the salad.
Serves 4

lima bean salad

Tinned lima beans are available from all good delis. You could also use most other kinds of tinned beans for this salad.

Ingredients

1 x 375g (13oz) tin lima beans, drained
4 whole spring onions, finely chopped
2 tomatoes, diced
3 sprigs of parsley, finely chopped
drizzle of olive oil
splash of brown malt vinegar
salt
pepper

Method

In a salad bowl, combine beans, spring onions, tomatoes and parsley and season with salt and pepper to taste.

Dress the salad with a small drizzle of olive oil and splash of vinegar.
Serves 4

Aristos' Tip: After dressing a salad I always run my hand under the cold water tap and flick the salad with the water to break down the acidity of the vinegar in the salad. This is something my mother taught me.

the boys tomato and
onion salad

pepperoni salad with
avocado dressing

pepperoni salad with avocado dressing

Ingredients

Salad

1 cos lettuce
150g (5½oz) snow peas
1 yellow capsicum, sliced
1 green capsicum, sliced
300g (10½oz) bean sprouts
60g (2oz) pepperoni salami, thinly
   sliced
12 croutons

Dressing

1 small avocado
125g (4½oz) cream cheese
½ cup (125ml/4½fl oz) French dressing
2 tablespoons lemon juice
2 tablespoons olive oil

Method

Tear lettuce into pieces and place in salad bowl. Add the snow peas, capsicum, bean sprouts, salami and croutons and toss together well.

To make the dressing, place the avocado, cream cheese, French dressing, lemon juice and olive oil in a blender and mix until smooth. Drizzle dressing over salad mix before serving.

Serves 4

caesar salad

Ingredients

Salad

1 rasher bacon, sliced
1 baby cos lettuce, washed and
   drained well
1 egg, soft boiled and cut into six
10g (½ oz) anchovies
30g (1oz) parmesan cheese, grated
12 croutons

Dressing

4 egg yolks
1 tablespoon seeded mustard
1 tablespoon Dijon mustard
100ml (3½fl oz) red wine vinegar
2 garlic cloves, crushed
100ml (3½fl oz) Worcestershire sauce
4 anchovy fillets
60g (2oz) Parmesan cheese, grated
500ml (17½fl oz) extra-virgin olive oil

Method

In a frying pan, sauté the bacon until crispy. Remove from heat and set aside.

Place cos leaves in a salad bowl. Add the soft boiled egg, bacon, anchovies, Parmesan and croutons.

To make dressing, place the egg yolks, seeded mustard, Dijon mustard, vinegar, garlic, Worcestershire sauce, anchovy fillets and Parmesan cheese in a blender and mix well. Gradually stir in the oil until a thick dressing forms. Drizzle over salad ingredients just before serving. Toss well.

Serves 4

thai noodle salad

Ingredients

Salad

500g (1lb) rice vermicelli noodles
2 cups carrots, julienned

Dressing

1 green chilli, finely chopped
3 tablespoons sweet chilli sauce
½ cup mint, finely chopped
½ cup basil, finely chopped
½ cup coriander, finely chopped
juice of 2 limes
¾ cup (6½fl oz) olive oil
⅓ cup (2fl oz) Thai fish sauce
2 tablespoons ABC sweet soy
  (available from Asian supermarkets)

Method

Cook noodles in a saucepan of boiling salted water until al dente. Rinse and drain. Put into serving dish with the carrots.

To make the dressing, in a bowl combine the chilli, chilli sauce, mint, basil, coriander, lime juice, olive oil, fish sauce and sweet soy and mix well.

Pour mixture over noodles and carrots. Toss well to coat.
Serves 4

dad's greek potato salad

Ingredients
2 potatoes, boiled
1 white onion, finely chopped
½ cup kalamata olives, pitted
drizzle of extra-virgin olive oil
splash of balsamic vinegar
2 eggs, boiled and quartered

Method
Dice the potatoes into 2cm (¾in) cubes.

In a salad bowl, combine the potatoes, onion and olives and toss well with the olive oil and vinegar. Arrange egg quarters on top of salad. Drizzle with a little more olive oil and season with salt and pepper to taste.
Serves 4

rocket salad

Ingredients
1 bunch of rocket, washed and
   drained well
2 Roma tomatoes, sliced
drizzle of olive oil
splash of balsamic vinegar
100g (3½oz) slivered almonds

Method
Tear rocket into pieces and place in a salad bowl with tomatoes.

To make the dressing, place the oil and vinegar in a bowl and whisk to combine well. Drizzle dressing over salad.

Place almonds in a hot frying pan to brown, stirring continuously so they do not burn. Sprinkle over top of salad just before serving.
Serves 4

greek salad

Anybody who tells you that a Greek salad has got iceberg lettuce in it doesn't know what they're talking about!

Ingredients
1 tomato, roughly chopped
2 small Lebanese cucumbers, sliced
12 kalamata olives
1 small white onion, roughly chopped
1 small red or green capsicum,
   roughly chopped
sprinkle of oregano
salt
pepper
drizzle of olive oil
splash of balsamic vinegar
100g (3½oz) feta cheese, preferably
   Dodoni, diced

Method
In a salad bowl, combine tomato, cucumbers, olives, onion, capsicum and a sprinkle of oregano. Season with salt and pepper to taste and toss well.

Drizzle with olive oil and a splash of balsamic vinegar. Sprinkle with water. Sprinkle the feta cubes over the top.
Serves 4

Aristos' Tip: This salad can be served with just about any food or as a simple lunch dish served with crusty bread.

dad's greek potato
salad

aristos' salad

aristos' salad

Ingredients

1 iceberg lettuce, washed, drained and
  shredded
2 Roma tomatoes, sliced
5 sundried tomato pieces
1 white onion, sliced
1 cucumber, diced

Dressing

6 anchovy fillets
12 capers
sprinkle of Parmesan cheese, grated
1 garlic clove
70ml (2½fl oz) lemon juice
1 teaspoon Dijon mustard
200ml (7fl oz) extra-virgin olive oil
salt
pepper

Method

Place lettuce, tomato, sundried tomato, onion and cucumber
in a salad bowl and mix well.

To make the dressing, place the anchovy fillets, capers,
cheese, garlic, lemon juice and mustard in a blender and
combine well. Slowly pour the oil into the mixture while
blending until a thick dressing forms. Season with salt and
pepper to taste.

Drizzle the dressing over the salad just before serving.

Serves 4

iceberg and fennel salad

Ingredients

1 large iceberg lettuce, washed,
  drained and torn into pieces
5 spring onions, finely chopped
small bunch of fennel or dill, finely
  chopped
drizzle of olive oil
juice of 1 lemon

Method

In a bowl, combine the lettuce, spring onions and fennel or dill
and toss well.

Drizzle with olive oil and lemon juice just before serving.

Serves 4

sauces

Like a cold beer, a good sauce can turn the mundane into memorable.

sauces

If you take a look into most professional kitchens, the one thing you'll see slowly cooking away somewhere is a sauce. It's the one pot you always go back to, check, give the contents a stir and maybe a taste, and then get on with whatever you were doing.

Chefs always have their own little variations on a sauce and there are all sorts of different names for them, but most are really based on just five "Mother Sauces". **They're not that hard to cook** and can make a world of difference to a meal.

The five basic sauces are: demiglaze, tomato Provençale, béchamel, velouté and hollandaise. While some, like the demiglaze, might take hours to prepare, others can be pulled together in less than ten minutes. Either way, a

good sauce will bring any meal to life. Think back to the last time you enjoyed a dish with a wonderful rich sauce: **You mopped it up with your bread** or whatever piece of food you had left on the plate. It was a sign that someone in the kitchen had done their job well.

The other easy way to give food a new twist is using butter. A simple garlic butter will take only a few minutes to prepare — that's no time at all if you're doing a barbecue. While everything is cooking on the hotplate, just take a step back and quickly make up the butter. Then, when the barbecued meat is ready, top it off with a small pat of homemade garlic butter and taste the difference — **fantastic!**

peppercorn sauce

Ingredients

30g (1oz) butter
1 tablespoon black or green
  peppercorns
50ml (2fl oz) Worcestershire sauce
1 teaspoon basil, chopped
1 teaspoon beef stock/demiglaze
  (recipe page 124)
60ml (2fl oz) brandy
100ml (3½fl oz) cream

Method

In a saucepan, melt the butter. Add the peppercorns,
Worcestershire sauce, basil, beef stock, brandy and cream.
Simmer over low heat until you have a thin sauce consistency.
If the sauce splits add a little cream and mix well.
Makes 250ml

béchamel sauce

Ingredients

60g (2oz) butter
60g (2oz) flour
1 small onion, peeled and studded
  with cloves
500ml (9fl oz) milk

Method

In a saucepan, prepare the roux by melting the butter and adding
the flour. Cook for 3 minutes and leave to cool, otherwise the
sauce will become lumpy.

In a separate saucepan, place the onion in the milk and heat
gently. Do not allow to boil. Remove onion and, over low heat,
pour the milk into the roux a little at a time, stirring continuously
for 10 minutes to prevent sauce sticking. Strain through a sieve
to remove any lumps and drizzle some melted butter on top of
the sauce to stop a skin from forming.

If the sauce is too thick add a little more milk to achieve the
right consistency. If the sauce is too thin, make a little more roux
and add to thicken.
Makes 600ml

Aristos' Tip: This sauce has a number of uses including
lasagna (recipe page 62) and crepe filling. By adding a little
Parmesan cheese, it becomes a delicious mornay sauce
perfect for topping grilled seafood.

aristos' red wine jus

Ingredients

60g (2oz) butter
6 shallots, finely chopped
100g (3½oz) button mushrooms, finely
  chopped
250ml (9fl oz) dry red wine
zest of 1 orange
250ml (9fl oz) beef stock/demiglaze
  (recipe page 124)
1 sprig of fresh rosemary
salt
pepper

Method

In a saucepan, melt the butter and sauté the shallots and
mushrooms for about 3 minutes or until soft. Add the wine and
orange zest and simmer until the liquid has reduced by one third.
Add the stock and rosemary simmer for 30 minutes.

Pass through sieve and, while hot, whisk in the remaining
butter. Season with salt and pepper to taste.

Serve with roast lamb or beef.
Makes 300ml

peppercorn sauce

tomato provençale

tomato provencale

Ingredients
2 x 400g (14oz) tins whole peeled
  tomatoes
handful of basil, chopped
2 garlic cloves, crushed
10g (½oz) oregano
splash of olive oil
salt
pepper

Method
In a saucepan, cook tomatoes, basil, garlic, oregano and olive oil on medium heat for 20 minutes, stirring occasionally. Season with salt and pepper to taste. Remove saucepan from heat and place through moulie or blender.
Makes 700ml

Aristos' Tip: This sauce can be used for any dish with a tomato base, such as soups and sauces. It can also be frozen for use at a later date.

janice's cacciatore sauce

Jan and Victor Kailis have been good friends of mine for a long time. Jan is a terrific cook – she has to be because Victor is very fussy! I normally make this sauce in bulk and keep it in the fridge, as I seem to use it all the time.

Ingredients
2 medium finger eggplants
4 tablespoons olive oil
2 large brown onions, finely chopped
4 garlic cloves, roughly chopped
1 red capsicum, diced
1 small zucchini, diced
10 small mushrooms, quartered
12 kalamata olives, pitted
2 x 375g (13oz) tins crushed tomatoes
½ cup fresh oregano
⅓ cup fresh parsley
½ cup fresh basil
pinch of sugar
salt
pepper

Method
Cut the eggplants in half lengthways and sprinkle with salt. Rest for 5 minutes and pat dry. Dice into 3cm (¼in) cubes and set aside.

In a large non-stick frying pan, heat the oil and sauté the onions and garlic until soft. Add the eggplant and capsicum and cook for 3 minutes, continuously stirring. Add the zucchini, mushrooms and olives and cook for a further 3 minutes on high heat or until the vegetables begin to soften. Add the tomatoes, oregano, parsley, basil, sugar and water and combine well. Season with salt and pepper to taste and simmer for about 30 minutes.

If the sauce is a little thin, simmer for a further 5 minutes or until the sauce thickens. Refrigerate or freeze until required.

Serve with steak or schnitzel.
Makes 500ml

Aristos' Tip: Fresh, over-ripe tomatoes can be also be used instead of tinned tomatoes. I usually grate them with a cheese grater.

cocktail sauce

Ingredients
300ml (10½fl oz) tomato sauce
100ml (3½fl oz) Worcestershire sauce
90ml (3fl oz) brandy
30ml (1fl oz) Tabasco
30ml (1fl oz) lemon juice
300ml (10½fl oz) mayonnaise
salt
pepper

Method
To make the sauce, combine the tomato sauce, Worcestershire sauce, brandy, Tabasco and lemon juice in a bowl and mix well. Add the mayonnaise and mix well until it is a nice thick consistency. Season with salt and pepper to taste.
Makes 850ml

Clockwise from top:
red pepper sauce,
mayonnaise,
mushroom sauce,
fresh tomato and
chilli salsa

coriander & mint chutney

Ingredients
3 bunches of coriander
1 bunch of mint
6–8 green chillies
6 garlic cloves
2 tablespoons lemon juice
1 tablespoon sugar
4cm (1½in) fresh ginger
2 tablespoons water
salt

Method
In a food processor, mix coriander, mint, chillies, garlic, lemon juice, sugar and ginger and blend to a paste. Add water and season with salt to taste.
Serves 4

Aristos' Tip: Serve with pakoras, samosas, meatballs, cold chicken or a platter of crudités. This chutney will keep for up to 6 months if sealed in sterilised airtight containers and stored in the fridge.

red pepper sauce

Ingredients
60g (2oz) butter
1 onion, finely chopped
2 celery stalks, finely chopped
3 red capsicum, finely chopped
1 small green chilli finely chopped or
 ½ teaspoon hot chilli powder
500g (1lb) tomatoes, coarsly chopped
2 sprigs of thyme
salt
pepper
1 sprig basil, finely chopped, to serve

Method
In a saucepan, melt butter and sauté the onion, celery, capsicum and chilli until tender. Add tomatoes, thyme and season with salt and pepper to taste. Simmer uncovered until mixture thickens. Sprinkle with basil and serve.
Makes 500ml

Aristos' Tip: This sauce is excellent with grilled steak, lamb chops or chicken breasts.

fresh tomato and chilli salsa

Ingredients
4 tomatoes, peeled, seeded and finely
 chopped
1 red chilli, seeded and finely chopped
3 tablespoons coriander, chopped
½ onion, finely chopped
1 garlic clove, crushed
3 teaspoons olive oil
3 teaspoons lemon juice
salt
pepper

Method
In a bowl, combine tomatoes, chilli, coriander, onion, garlic, olive oil and lemon juice and mix well. Season with salt and pepper to taste. Use straightaway or store in the fridge.
Serves 4

Aristos' Tip: Serve this salsa with tacos or as a topping on grilled fish, chicken or vegetables.

desserts

tartare sauce

Ingredients

150g (5½oz) gherkins, sliced
100g (3½oz) capers
100g (3½oz) onions, roughly chopped
20ml gherkin juice
25ml caper juice
60g (2oz) parsley, chopped
60g (2oz) tinned anchovy fillets,
  drained and chopped
juice of ½ a lemon
700ml (1¼pint) mayonnaise
  (recipe page 123)

Method

Place the gherkins, capers, onions, gherkin juice, caper juice, parsley, anchovy and lemon juice in a blender and mix thoroughly. Add home-made or ready-made mayonnaise and combine well.

Serve with crumbed fish or fried or grilled seafood.
Makes 750ml

sweet chilli sauce

Ingredients

750ml (1¼ pints) sweet chilli sauce
200ml (7fl oz) rice wine vinegar
100g (3½oz) coriander, chopped
100g (3½oz) mint, chopped
100g (3½fl oz) water
½cup (125g/4½oz) sugar

Method

In a bowl, mix sweet chilli sauce, vinegar, coriander, mint, water and sugar and combine well. This sauce may be kept in a sterilised bottle in the refrigerator for up to 3 months.

This sauce is ideal with Jamaican fish cakes (recipe page 26) or fish and chips.
Make 1l

dianne sauce

Ingredients

60g (2oz) butter
1 onion, diced
100ml (3½fl oz) Worcestershire sauce
1 teaspoon basil, finely chopped
100ml (3½fl oz) beef stock demiglaze
  (recipe page 124)
100ml (3½fl oz) cream
60ml (2oz) brandy

Method

Melt butter in a saucepan and sauté onion without colouring. Add basil, Worcestershire sauce, beef stock, cream and brandy. Reduce until sauce thickens. If the sauce splits add a little more cream. Serve with steak or barbecued meat.
Makes 300ml

Aristos' Tip: Reducing not only thickens the consistency of the sauce but it also creates a stronger flavour.

anchovy butter

Ingredients

250g (9oz) butter, softened
100g (3½oz) anchovy fillets, finely
  chopped
pepper

Method

Place butter, anchovies and a pinch of pepper in a bowl and mix well or place in a food processor for 3 minutes until well combined.

Mould the butter into a sausage shape and wrap it in plastic wrap. Refrigerate until ready to use.

Aristos' Tip: To serve, slice off a small piece of the butter and place inside some barbecued fish while it's still hot.

tartare sauce

Sundried capsicum
and tomato salsa

sundried capsicum and tomato salsa

Ingredients

100g (3½oz) sundried capsicum in olive oil, drained and chopped
250g (9oz) yellow teardrop tomatoes, quartered
3 tablespoons basil, chopped
2 teaspoons sundried capsicum oil
pepper

Method

In a bowl, combine capsicum, tomatoes, basil and oil and mix well. Season to taste with pepper. Serve on toasted bread slices as bruschetta or with barbecued sausages, lamb chops or chicken.
Serves 4-6

Aristos' Tip: I like to toast some slices of bread and drizzle them with extra-virgin olive oil. I then grate a Roma tomato into a bowl, season to taste with salt and pepper and smear it over the bread.

beef stock/demiglaze

Ingredients

1kg (2lb) beef bones
1kg (2lb) veal bones
1kg (2lb) chicken bones
500g (1lb) stewing beef
2 carrots
2 onions
2 celery sticks
sprinkle of peppercorns
10l (16½ pints) water

Method

Place the bones, stewing beef, carrots, onions, celery sticks, peppercorns and water in a large pot. Bring to the boil slowly and skim the top thoroughly. Simmer gently for 7 to 8 hours. Strain, return to the pot and rapid boil until reduced by a third.
Makes 3l

Aristos' Tip: This is a general-purpose brown stock which can be used on its own or as a base to widen the repertoire of any kitchen, particularly to enhance casseroles, pies and sautéed mushrooms.

mum's home-made tomato sauce

I am a big fan of tomato sauce, especially with a good shepherd's pie or home-made sausage rolls. This recipe was too good to leave out!

Ingredients

2kg (4lb) tomatoes, chopped
500g (1lb) sugar
1 teaspoon white pepper, ground
2 garlic cloves, finely chopped
1 teaspoon whole black peppercorns
4 teaspoons salt
75ml (2½fl oz) brown malt vinegar
1 teaspoon whole cloves
1 chilli, roughly chopped
2 granny smith apples, cored, peeled and chopped
3 brown onions, roughly chopped

Method

Place all the ingredients in a large saucepan and combine well. Bring to the boil and reduce heat. Check often and stir occasionally. Simmer for 3 hours.

Sterilise storage jars by boiling them in water or pouring boiling water into them. Strain the sauce through a sieve and into the jars immediately, while both the sauce and the jars are still hot.
Fills 2-3 500ml jars

hollandaise sauce

Ingredients
300g (10½oz) butter
75ml (2½fl oz) white vinegar
1 tablespoon water
12 peppercorns
3 egg yolks
juice of 1 lemon
salt
pepper

Method
To clarify the butter, melt the butter in a saucepan and allow to separate. Pour off melted butter and set aside. Discard the milk solids.

In a separate saucepan, simmer vinegar, water and peppercorns into a pan. Simmer until reduced to one third. Allow to cool and, over a double boiler, add the egg yolks. Whisk until creamy and remove from heat.

Drizzle in the clarified butter, a little at a time, whisking well. When all butter is incorporated and the mixture is creamy, add the lemon juice and season with salt and pepper to taste. Use as required.
Makes 300ml

Aristos' Tip: If the sauce begins to curdle, place the pot over some ice and keep whisking. Remove from ice when curdling is corrected.

mayonnaise

Ingredients
7 egg yolks
60ml (2fl oz) white vinegar
1 dessertspoon Dijon mustard
1 dessertspoon seeded mustard
1 tablespoon lemon juice
1l (1⅔ pints) good-quality vegetable oil
salt
pepper
60ml (2fl oz) hot water, optional

Method
Whisk together egg yolks, vinegar, both mustards and lemon juice using an electric mixer with a whisk attachment, or by hand, until well combined. Very slowly, add a little oil at a time, whisking continuously until all the oil is incorporated and the consistency is thick. Season to taste with salt and pepper.

If the consistency is too thick, add a little hot water to adjust.
Makes 1l

mushroom sauce

Ingredients
80g (3oz) butter
2 cups mushrooms, chopped
60ml (2fl oz) Worcestershire sauce
100ml (3½fl oz) cream
salt
pepper

Method
Melt butter in pan and sauté the mushrooms for 2 minutes on high heat. Add Worcestershire sauce and cream and simmer until sauce thickens. If the sauce splits, add a little more cream and mix well.

Season with salt and pepper.
Makes 250ml

Aristos' Tip: This sauce is great with barbecued meat or crumbed meat.

hollandaise sauce

coriander & mint
chutney

desserts

For a long time desserts were not my strong point — mainly because you have to measure so precisely, using half a teaspoon of this, half an ounce of that, and I really prefer throwing in a bit of whatever takes my fancy as I go! You can't get away with that in a dessert, so it was always the one course that frustrated me.

Then out of the blue I was asked to be guest chef at a dinner at a winery in Western Australia. I had to create the entire menu, including dessert. As usual I couldn't think of what to do so I called the chef who usually runs the winery kitchen and told her I'd be honoured if she'd make dessert; anything she liked. After all, I was entering her domain. Unfortunately for me, she said she wouldn't dream of interfering ... It was time for that reliable old SOS call: **"Mum! Help!"**

Mum has rescued me in the kitchen on more than one occasion!

A couple of days later, a package arrived from mum with some recipe suggestions. I happened to be out at a Chinese restaurant and was running through some of the ideas when **the proverbial lightbulb flashed over my head** and the solution hit me.

I made some spring rolls, stuffed them with feta, ricotta and apricots, then made a blackberry sauce to pour over the top, sprinkled with a bit of icing sugar. I was really making it up as I went and had no idea how it would turn out. But when it was ready I took a bite, and you know what? **It was magnificent!**

baked banana slice

Ingredients
1 cup self raising flour
½ cup sugar, extra
60g (2oz) butter
1 egg, beaten
⅓ cup milk
1 teaspoon lemon zest
½ teaspoon cinnamon
butter, melted, for glazing
3 medium-size bananas, peeled and
  sliced

Method
Preheat oven to 180°C (350°F)

In a bowl, sift flour and combine with sugar. Rub in the butter with your fingertips and add the egg and milk. Stir until well blended. Spread the mixture evenly into a greased 28cm (11in) x 18cm (7in) lamington tin.

In a bowl, combine an extra tablespoon of sugar, lemon zest and cinnamon in a bowl and sprinkle over the mixture in the tin. Arrange the bananas on top and brush with melted butter.

Bake for 30–35 mins or until golden brown.

To serve, cut into squares and serve with whipped cream or custard.

Serves 10

banana and bourbon

Ingredients
4 bananas, medium–ripe
100g (3½oz) butter
2 tablespoons brown sugar
90ml (3fl oz) Jack Daniels or Jim Beam
  bourbon

Method
Peel bananas and slice diagonally. In a non-stick frying pan, melt butter and sugar and stir until dissolved. Add bananas and lightly sauté for about 2 minutes each side. Add bourbon.

Serve with cream or ice cream.

Serves 4

aristos' apple strudel

Ingredients
50g (2oz) butter
6 large granny smith apples, peeled,
  cored and diced
150g (5½oz) sultanas
60ml (2fl oz) brandy or cognac
2 tablespoons sugar
2 tablespoons cinnamon, ground
2 sheets puff pastry
1 egg yolk

Method
Preheat oven to 180°C (350°F).

In a medium saucepan, heat the butter and add the apples and sultanas. Sauté until apples begin to soften. Add the brandy and remove from heat. Add the sugar and cinnamon immediately and mix well. Allow to cool.

Spoon half the mixture onto the right side of one pastry sheet and fold the left side over the mixture so the two edges meet. Trim the pastry so that it looks like an even rectangle. To seal the strudel, press the pastry edges down with a fork ensuring there are no gaps.

Make another strudel with the remaining pastry sheet and mixture.

Brush the egg yolk over the two strudels and place them in a baking tray. Bake strudels for about 20 minutes or until golden brown.

Serve hot with ice cream or freshly whipped cream.

Serves 8

Baked banana slice

granny's apple pie

Grandmas always seem to make the best apple pie. Everytime my uncles and I would visit Nanna's house we would go straight to the electric oven and open the door because that's where we'd find any leftover apple pie!

Ingredients

Pastry
250g plain flour
125g (4½oz) butter, softened
water
flour, for kneading

Filling
60g (2oz) butter
5 Granny Smith apples, peeled, cored and sliced
½ cup sultanas
1 tablespoon sugar
1 teaspoon cinnamon
splash of brandy or apple brandy

Method

To make the pastry, mix the butter and flour in a bowl using your fingertips so that the mixture becomes crumbly. Gradually add water until the mixture becomes a soft dough. Sprinkle a little flour on your bench surface and knead the dough.

Divide the dough in two, one piece slightly larger than the other. Flatten the dough and sprinkle some flour on top to stop the rolling pin sticking. Roll the larger piece of dough out thinly so it is large enough to cover the base of a pie dish. Roll out the rest of the dough to make the lid of the pie. Grease the pie dish and sprinkle enough flour to cover the base of the dish. Lay the dough into the bowl and cut around the edge, removing any excess pastry.

Preheat oven to 200°C (400°F). To make the filling, heat some butter in a pan and sauté the apples and sultanas and add a splash of brandy. Allow to simmer for around 5–10 minutes, being careful not to overcook the apples.

In a small bowl combine the sugar and cinnamon. Remove the saucepan from the heat and add half the cinnamon and sugar mixture. (Don't attempt this while the apple mixture is still cooking as they apples and sultanas will stick to the bottom of the pan.) Mix well and pour the filling into the pie dish. Place the pastry lid over the top of the filling and cut off any excess pastry. Join the base and lid by pushing down around the rim with a fork.

Bake the pie for about 15–20 minutes or until top is golden brown. Remove pie from oven and sprinkle some cinnamon sugar over the top.

Serve with cream, ice cream or custard.

Serves 6

three fruit cassata

Ingredients

1½l (2½ pints) vanilla ice cream
1 x 375g (13oz) tin mango slices, drained
1 x 375g (13oz) jar moreschino cherries, drained and chopped
30ml (1fl oz) strawberry liqueur
150g (5½oz) coconut, shredded

Method

Partly defrost ice cream so that it can be divided easily into three equal portions.

Blend the mango slices in blender and mix through one-third of the ice cream. Pour the mixture into an empty 2l (3½pints) ice cream container or similar, and put into freezer to harden.

In a bowl, combine the cherries with the strawberry liqueur. Mix the cherry mixture through another third of the ice cream. When the mango ice cream is hard, pour the cherry mixture on top and return to freezer to harden.

Finally, combine the remaining ice cream with the coconut and mix well. When the cherry ice cream has hardened, pour the coconut mixture on top and return to the freezer to harden.

Serve when all the layers are hard.

Serves 10-12

easy boiled chocolate cake

Ingredients

Cake

1 cup sugar
100g (3½oz) butter
1 cup (250ml/9fl oz) water
2 tablespoons cocoa powder
1 teaspoon bicarbonate of soda
2 eggs, beaten
1½ cups self raising flour

Icing

1 cup icing sugar
3 tablespoons cocoa
water

Method

Preheat oven to 180°C (350°F).

In a saucepan, mix sugar, butter, water and cocoa and bring to the boil. Mix in bicarbonate of soda and allow to cool. Stir in eggs and sifted flour and combine well. Pour mixture into a greased cake tin and bake for 40–45 minutes or until cooked through; a skewer inserted into cake should come out clean. Allow to cool.

To make the icing, combine the icing sugar and cocoa in a bowl with enough water to make a smooth paste. Evenly distribute the icing over the cake.

Serve with whipped cream and strawberries.

Serves 4

Three fruit cassata

Mascarpone surprise

mascarpone surprise

Ingredients

250g (9oz) mascarpone cheese
2 tablespoons sugar
½ cup berries, blackberries,
  strawberries or blueberries
60ml (2fl oz) Cointreau
juice of ½ lemon
1 meringue shell, pre-cooked

Method

In a bowl, beat the mascarpone until soft. Add half the sugar and mix well.

In another bowl, mix berries, Cointreau, lemon juice and the rest of sugar and allow to sit for 1 hour.

In a martini or parfait glass, place a layer of mascarpone mixture followed by the berry mixture. Repeat until the mixtures reach the top of the glass. Crumble the meringue on top.
Serves 2

apples calvados

Ingredients

2 granny smith apples, cored, peeled
  and diced
3 pears, peeled and cut into quarters
60g (2oz) of sultanas
60g (2oz) butter
1 clove
1 teaspoon of sugar
zest of 1 lemon, optional
30ml (1fl oz) Calvados, hospital
  brandy or cognac
ice cream, to serve
wafers, to serve

Method

In a saucepan, melt the butter and add the apples, pears, sultanas, clove, sugar and lemon zest. Place the lid on the saucepan and simmer the mixture on low heat until the apples are soft. Add the brandy and remove from heat.

Spoon the fruit into individual bowls and serve immediately with vanilla ice cream and wafers.

This can also be refrigerated and served cold with custard.
Serves 4

beginner's luck strawberries and cream

When I first started cooking for girls, I would always use this foolproof recipe to impress them and it never let me down!

Ingredients

1 punnet large strawberries, washed
  and drained
1 tablespoon sugar
30ml (1fl oz) cognac or brandy
1 small tub cream, preferably King
  Island

Method

Cut the tops off the strawberries and slice them in half from top to bottom. Place them in a bowl and add the sugar and brandy. Toss well and refrigerate for 1 hour.

To serve, divide the strawberries between two martini glasses and drizzle the juice from the strawberries over the top. Serve with a good dollop of cream.
Serves 2

cinnamon sour cream cake

Ingredients

1 cup butter
1¼ cups sugar
2 eggs
1 cup sour cream
2 cups plain flour
½ teaspoon baking soda
1½ teaspoon baking powder
1 teaspoons vanilla essence
¾ cup walnuts, finely chopped
1 teaspoon cinnamon
2 tablespoons sugar, for topping

Method

In a large bowl, mix butter, sugar and eggs and beat until light and fluffy. Fold in the sour cream. Sift flour, soda and baking powder into mixture and combine well. Add the vanilla essence and blend well. Spoon half the batter into a 23cm (9in) cake or loaf tin which has been greased and floured.

In a small bowl, combine walnuts, cinnamon and sugar together and sprinkle half of this mixture onto the batter in the cake tin. Spoon the remaining batter into the cake tin and top with the rest of the walnut mixture.

Place in cold oven and bake at 180°C (350°F) for about 55 minutes until the top is golden brown and a skewer inserted into the cake comes out clean.

Serves 8

my brother stathy's cheese scones

Ingredients

2 cups cheese, grated
2 cups self raising flour, sifted
2 cups (17½fl oz) milk
½ teaspoon cayenne pepper

Method

Preheat oven to 180°C (350°F).

In a bowl, combine cheese, flour and milk and mix well until a soft dough is achieved. Spoon the mixture into greased muffin pan and bake for 20–25 minutes or until the scones are light and fluffy.

Makes 6

crème brulée

Ingredients

500ml (17½fl oz) cream
500ml (17½fl oz) milk
1 vanilla bean
8 egg yolks
¾ cup sugar
4 tablespoons brown sugar

Method

Preheat oven to 190°C (375°F). In a saucepan, warm the cream, milk and vanilla bean for 5 minutes.

In a bowl, whisk the egg yolks and sugar together and gradually stir the cream mixture into the egg mixture and combine well. Strain the custard into another bowl and skim off the bubbles. Spoon the custard mixture into eight 10cm (4in) x 15cm (6in) oval dishes.

Fill half a large baking tray with boiling water and place dishes into the tray. Cover loosely with aluminium foil and bake for 1 hour or until the custard is set but still wiggles a little.

Just before serving, sprinkle a thin layer of brown sugar over the custard and place under the grill for 30 seconds to 2 minutes, watching it closely to ensure the sugar does not burn. Remove from grill when the sugar is caramelized and golden brown.

Serves 6-8

Cinnamon sour
cream cake

panna cotta with forest berries

Ingredients

3 teaspoons gelatine
310ml (10½fl oz) milk
500ml (17½fl oz) thickened cream
165g (5½oz) sugar
2 teaspoons vanilla essence
assorted berries: strawberries,
   blueberries and blackberries
mint sprigs

Method

Sprinkle gelatine over 60ml (2fl oz) of milk and stir well. Allow to stand for 5 minutes.

In a saucepan, combine the remaining milk with the cream and sugar and gently heat without boiling. Remove from heat and stir in gelatine mixture, then add the vanilla essence. Strain into a jug. Pour mixture into six 180ml (6oz) dishes and refrigerate for 3 hours.

When the mixture has set, turn each panna cotta onto individual chilled plates and scatter with assorted berries. Garnish with sprigs of mint.

Serves 6

Aristos' Tip: Panna cotta can be made with any fruit you happen to have, such as peaches and nectarines.

Custard slice

custard slice

Ingredients

375g (13oz) filo pastry
125g (4½oz) butter, melted
4 eggs, beaten
1 cup (250ml/9fl oz) milk
1 cup sugar

Method

Preheat oven to 190°C (375°F).

Gently scrunch each sheet of filo and place in a 33cm (13in) x 25cm (10in) baking dish, starting at the centre until the pastry covers the whole tray. Drizzle the pastry with butter and cook for 15 minutes or until golden brown in colour. Remove from oven and set aside.

In a bowl, mix eggs, milk and sugar together until well combined. Pour mixture over the filo pastry and cook for another 10 minutes or until set. Remove from oven and leave to cool in the baking dish.

To serve, dust the slice with icing sugar.

Serves 6-8

crème caramel

I like to make a few extra of these because they are great to eat at any time of the day, not just after dinner.

Ingredients

1l (1⅔pints) milk
6 eggs
4 egg yolks
120g (4oz) sugar
2 teaspoons vanilla essence
200g (7oz) sugar
130ml (4½fl oz) water

Method

Preheat oven to 180°C (350°F).

To make the caramel, heat 100ml (3½fl oz) of water and the sugar in a small saucepan. Bring to the boil and cook until the syrup is a caramel colour. Add the remaining cold water to stop the caramel from cooking and cover the bottom of 10 dariole moulds with the caramel. Set aside and allow to set.

In a saucepan, heat the milk. Do not boil.

In a bowl, mix the eggs, egg yolks and vanilla essence and combine well. Slowly add the milk, stirring constantly, until well combined.

Half fill a large baking tray with hot water. Fill the dariole moulds with the mixture and place in the baking tray. Place the tray in the oven and cook for about 40 minutes.

When cooked, remove dariole moulds from the oven and refrigerate for about 2 hours or until set.

To serve, loosen the top edges of the caramel by softly pushing down on the crème caramel with your fingers. Place a flat plate on top of mould and, holding the mould and plate tightly together, turn the mould upside down and shake once.

Serve with fresh cream and peeled orange.

Serves 10

mum's kourambiethes (greek shortbread)

Ingredients
250g (9oz) butter
3 tablespoons icing sugar
1 egg yolk
½ cup toasted almonds, chopped
2 tablespoons ouzo or brandy
3 cups plain flour
1 teaspoon baking powder
icing sugar, for topping

Method
Preheat oven to 180°C (350°F). In a bowl, beat together the butter and icing sugar. Add egg yolk and combine well. Stir in almonds and ouzo. Gradually add flour and baking powder sifted together and mix well until the mixture becomes a soft dough.

Roll the dough into balls and pat them down with your hand. Place the shortbread on an ungreased baking tray and bake in a 180°C (350°F) oven for 15 minutes or until light golden in colour. Turn oven off and leave shortbread in for a further 5 minutes. When cool, sift over icing sugar.
Makes 24

pancakes

Ingredients
250g self raising flour
salt
2 eggs, beaten
500ml (17½fl oz) milk
oil or butter

Method
Sift flour and salt into a bowl. Make a well in the centre. Add eggs and slowly add the milk to the dry ingredients. Beat until you have a smooth batter.

In a heavy-based frying pan heat a little oil or butter until hot. Tip out excess oil and pour a thin layer of batter to coat the bottom of pan. Cook both sides until golden. Repeat until mixture is finished.

Pancakes can be served with a sprinkle of cinnamon, sugar and a squeeze of lemon or filled with fruit and custard, either flat or rolled-up.

Aristos' Tip: For savoury pancakes, sauté some prawn meat and combine well with béchamel sauce (recipe page 114). Fold into a parcel and serve as an entrée.

Mum's
kourumbiethes
(greek shortbread)

Ingredients

7 cups raspberries, frozen or fresh
¾ cup sugar
1 loaf white bread, sliced and crusts removed
2 tablespoons raspberry jam
1 tablespoon water, warm
¼ cup (50ml/2fl oz) thickened cream, whipped
4 mint leaves

Method

Mash 5 cups of raspberries with the sugar until the berries are half liquefied.

Line the bottom of a round 12cm (5in) diameter cake tin with a sheet of plastic wrap, leaving enough hanging over the sides to cover the top of the pudding later on. Coat the bottom of the pan with a very thin layer of the liquefied raspberries. Place a layer of bread over the berries, carefully fitting the slices together. Repeat until you have 3 layers of bread alternating with 4 layers of raspberries. Cover the top of the cake with the reserved plastic wrap. Place a weight on top and refrigerate overnight.

When ready to serve, gently knock the bottom of the pan to loosen the pudding and carefully remove the plastic wrap.

In a bowl, combine the raspberry jam with warm water. Very gently, stir the remaining 2 cups of raspberries into the melted raspberry jam. Cover the top of the pudding with the raspberry mixture.

Serve with whipped cream and fresh mint leaves.

Serves 4

Snow-white
chocolate
strawberries

snow-white chocolate strawberries

Ingredients

200g (7oz) coveture white cooking
  chocolate
12 large strawberries, washed

Method

Place chocolate pieces in a glass bowl over a pan of
simmering water and heat gently, stirring continuously. When
chocolate has melted, half dip each strawberry in chocolate
and place on a large plate covered with greaseproof paper.
    Place in the fridge immediately until ready to serve.

Serves 2

Aristos' Tip: Do not overcook the chocolate, as it will lose
its runny consistency.

raspberry mousse

Ingredients

4 eggs
1 cup (250ml/9fl oz) milk
3 tablespoons sugar
1 tablespoon sweet sherry
½ teaspoon vanilla essence
2 cups tinned raspberries, drained
  and crushed
2 cups (500ml/9fl oz) cream, whipped

Method

Separate eggs, keeping both yolks and whites. Beat egg yolks.
Heat milk, egg yolks and sugar in the top of a double boiler.
Stir continuously until custard coats the spoon. Remove from
heat and beat in sherry and vanilla essence. Leave to cool.
Add the raspberries and mix in gently.
    In a separate bowl, beat the egg whites until stiff. Fold the
egg whites into raspberry mixture. Gently fold the cream into
the mixture. Pour the mixture into individual serving dishes
and chill for 3 or 4 hours.

Serves 4-6

fresh custard dessert

Ingredients

2 large egg yolks
30g (1oz) sugar
300ml (10½fl oz) milk
1 teaspoon vanilla essence

Method

In a bowl, whisk the eggs and sugar.
    In a saucepan, heat the milk until boiling. Gently stir the milk
into the egg mixture until well combined. Return the mixture to
the saucepan and place on very low heat and stir continuously
with a wooden spoon until the custard coats the back of the
spoon. Do not allow to boil.
    Strain the custard through a fine sieve and gently stir in the
vanilla essence until well combined.

Serves 4

ravani (greek sugar cake)

Ingredients

3 cups (1¼pints) water
2¾ cups sugar
juice of ½ orange
250g (9oz) butter, melted
5 eggs, beaten
2 teaspoons vanilla essence
2 cups self raising flour
1 cup semolina
3 teaspoons baking powder
½ cup (125ml/4½fl oz) cream, whipped
¼ cup walnuts, chopped

Method

Preheat oven to 180°C (350°F).

To make the syrup, boil the water, 2 cups of sugar and orange juice over medium heat for 15 minutes. Set aside and cool.

To make the cake, pour the melted butter into a bowl and add the remaining sugar. Stir until the sugar dissolves. Add the eggs, mixing well, and stir in the vanilla essence. Mix the flour, semolina and baking powder and sift into the egg mixture. Combine well.

Pour mixture into a 36cm (14in) x 25cm(10in) cake tin and bake for 35 minutes or until the cake is cooked; a skewer inserted into the cake should come out clean. Remove from oven and pour the syrup over the cake while still hot. Allow to cool in cake tin.

Serve with whipped cream and sprinkle with walnuts.

Serves 10-12

rizogalo (greek rice pudding)

I think my mother makes the best rizogalo in the world. It was only when I asked her to teach me that she told me it was actually aunty Val's recipe. (See, I told you my aunty Val made the tastiest treats!)

Ingredients

⅓ cup short-grain white rice
½ cup water
1l (1⅔ pints) milk
2 egg yolks
½ cup sugar
salt
zest of 1 lemon
2 teaspoons vanilla essence
pinch cinnamon, ground

Method

In a saucepan, boil the rice in the water for 5 minutes. Remove saucepan from heat and strain.

In a separate saucepan, heat the milk. Do not allow to boil. Add the rice and simmer over low heat for 45 minutes, stirring occasionally. Remove the saucepan from heat and set aside.

In a bowl, whisk the egg yolks, sugar and a pinch of salt until well combined. Slowly stir the egg mixture into the rice and cook over low heat until the mixture is creamy and thick.

Add the vanilla essence and lemon zest and mix well.

Fill individual dessert bowls or martini glasses with rice pudding and sprinkle with cinnamon. Refrigerate for about 2 hours or until set.

Serve cold with coffee and port.

Serves 4–6

strawberries & ice cream

Ingredients

2 punnets strawberries, washed
2 tablespoons sugar
60ml (2fl oz) brandy
8 scoops vanilla ice cream
150ml (5½fl oz) cream, whipped

Method

Cut the tops off the strawberries and slice in half. In a bowl, mix the strawberries with sugar and brandy and leave to stand for 1 hour.

To serve, spoon strawberries into martini glass and top with ice cream and cream.

Serves 4–6

Ravani (greek sugar cake)

index

index

credits

Page 15 "Onnellinen" fabric by Marimekko, Chee Soon & Fitzgerald. Three-pod serving platter, Empire Homewares. Pâté knife, The Bay Tree.

Page 16 Long white platter, The Bay Tree. Small white bowl, Ikea. Small square plate and striped napkin, Orson & Blake.

Page 18-19 Bowl, Empire Homewares. Soup spoons and Plantation paprika napkin, The Bay Tree. Chinese chopping block, Burlington Centre Chinatown.

Page 21 Square white plate, Orson & Blake. Green kidney plate, Mitchell + Helen English. Olive oil bottle, stylist's own.

Page 22 Red and white tea towel, The Bay Tree.

Page 24-25 Side plates and small bowl, Empire Homewares. Fringed napkins, Country Road Homewares. Chopping block, Major & Tom. Fork, The Bay Tree.

Page 27 Glass platter and small glass dipping bowl, Orrefors Kosta Boda. Striped napkin, Orson & Blake.

Page 28 White ramekins, stylist's own. Rectangular dish, Ikea. Orange napkin, Country Road Homewares. Fork, The Bay Tree.

Page 30-31 Pandan placemat and white linen napkin, Orson & Blake. Boda Nova "Tellus" crockery, Orrefors Kosta Boda.

Hackman fork, Empire Homewares.

Page 33 Tea towel, The Bay Tree. Beer glasses, Ikea.

Page 34 Fringed napkin, Country Road Homewares. Ceramic plates, Orson & Blake. George Jensen soup spoon, Orrefors Kosta Boda.

Page 43 Bowl, Empire Homewares. George Jensen "New York" fork, Orrefors Kosta Boda. Placemat, Orson & Blake.

Page 44 Wooden spatula, Ikea. Napkin, stylist's own.

Page 46-47 "Tellus" crockery, Orrefors Kosta Boda. Hackman cutlery, Empire Homewares. "Unikko" fabric by Marimekko, Chee Soon & Fitzgerald.

Page 49 Speckled bowl, Empire Homewares.

Page 50
"Da Vinci" bowl, Country Road Homewares. Tin of anchovies, D & K deli at Leichhardt.

Page 53 Wooden plate, Major & Tom. "Kude" fabric by Marimekko, Chee Soon & Fitzgerald.

Page 54 Mason and Cash ceramic bowl, The Essential Ingredient. White ceramic plate, Orson & Blake. Hackman spoon, Empire Homewares. Napkin, Lanterne/Ginger Flower.

Page 59 Dinner plates, Ikea. Napkin, Country Road Homewares. Cutlery, The Bay Tree.

Page 60 "Heina" fabric by Marimekko, Chee Soon & Fitzgerald. Tea towel, The Bay Tree. Le Creuset casserole dish, The Essential Ingredient.

Page 63 "Heina" fabric by Marimekko, Chee Soon & Fitzgerald. Mason and Cash casserole dish, The Essential Ingredient. Orange ceramic plate, Mitchell + Helen English. Hackman fork, Empire Homewares.

Page 64 Plate and bowl, Empire Homewares. Napkin, The Bay Tree.

Page 67 Plate and bowl, Empire Homewares.

Page 68 "Unikko" fabric by Marimekko, Chee Soon & Fitzgerald. Terracotta dish, The Essential Ingredient. Oven cloth, The Bay Tree.

Page 70-71 Large ceramic platter and ceramic bowl, Country Road Homewares. Carving set, The Essential Ingredient. Chopping board, Major & Tom.

Page 73 "Da Vinci" bowls, small condiment bowl and "Mare" napkin, all Country Road Homewares.

Page 74-75 "Space" plate and "Aria" bowl, Empire Homewares. Wooden spoon, Ikea. Napkin, Lanterne/Ginger Flower.

Page 76 Mason and Cash casserole dish, The Essential Ingredient. Ceramic plate,

Orson & Blake. Fork and salt container, The Bay Tree.

Page 79 Ceramic bowls and napkin, Country Road Homewares. George Jensen "New York" fork, Orrefors Kosta Boda. "Unikko" fabric by Marimekko, Chee Soon & Fitzgerald.

Page 80 Bowl, Empire Homewares.

Page 83 Le Creuset baking dish, The Essential Ingredient.

Page 89 Wooden bowls, Mitchell + Helen English. Wooden spoon, Ikea. Napkin, Orson & Blake. "Satula" fabric by Marimekko, Chee Soon & Fitzgerald.

Page 90 Bowl, Lanterne/Ginger Flower.

Page 92-93 Oven cloth, The Essential Ingredient. Baking dish, stylist's own.

Page 95 Rectangular platter, The Bay Tree. "Satula" fabric by Marimekko, Chee Soon & Fitzgerald.

Page 101 Square plate, Orson & Blake. Hackman fork, Empire Homewares. Napkin, Country Road Homewares.

Page 102 Glass salad bowl, Ikea. Spoon, The Bay Tree. Small Pyrex dish, The Chefs' Warehouse.

Page 104-105 Bowl, Lanterne/Ginger Flower.

stockists

Homewares

The Bay Tree
40 Holdsworth Street
Woollahra NSW 2025
Tel 02 9328 1101

Chee Soon & Fitzgerald
387 Crown Street
Surry Hills NSW 2010
Tel 02 9360 1031

The Chefs' Warehouse
252 Riley Street
Surry Hills NSW 2010
Tel: 02 9211 4555

Country Road Homewares
Level 2, Skygardens
Shopping Centre
213 Castlereagh Street
Sydney NSW 2000
Tel 02 9223 7985
Tel 1800 801 911 for
national branches

Empire Homewares
18-22 Oxford Street
Paddington NSW 2021
Tel 02 9380 8877

The Essential Ingredient
4-6 Australia Street
Camperdown NSW 2050
Tel 02 9550 5477

Ginger Flower
Shop 4,
3-9 Broughton Street
Kirribilli NSW 2061
Tel 02 8920 3199

Ikea
Supercentre
Cnr. South Dowling
Street & Todman Avenue
Moore Park NSW 2021
Tel 02 9313 6400

Lanterne
330 Victoria Street
Darlinghurst NSW 2010
Tel 02 9380 7172

Major & Tom
45 Barwon Park Road
St Peters NSW 2044
Tel 02 9557 8380

Mitchell + Helen English
Shop 8/2-16 Glenmore Rd
Paddington NSW 2021
Tel 02 9331 0075

Orrefors Kosta Boda
Shop L218
Chatswood Chase
Chatswood NSW 2067
Tel 02 9415 4912

Orson & Blake
483 Riley Street
Surry Hills NSW 2010
Tel 8399 2525

Produce
Barbaro Bros Quality Butchers
Shop 2,
120 Cockman Rd,
Greenwood WA 6064
Ph: 9247 4244

Demcos
ph 02 9700 9000

D & K Deli
Shop 19, Marketplace
Flat Street
Leichhardt NSW 2040
Tel 02 9560 8956

Murdoch Produce
Ph 02 9517 2018

T&R Gourmet Butchery
Shop 14
Cosmopolitan Centre
Double Bay 2028
ph 02 9327 6107

cooking with
aristos